Dictionary of Human Rights Advocacy Organizations in Africa

Santosh Saha

GREENWOOD PRESS
Westport, Connecticut • London

Library of Congress Cataloging-in-Publication Data

Saha, Santosh C.
　　Dictionary of human rights advocacy organizations in Africa /
Santosh Saha.
　　　　p.　　cm.
　　Includes bibliographical references and index.
　　ISBN 0–313–30945–0 (alk. paper)
　　1. Civil rights—Africa. 2. Human rights—Africa. 3. Nongovernmental organizations—Africa—Directories. 4. Associations,
institutions, etc.—Africa—Directories. I. Title.
JC599.A36S24　1999
323′.025′6—dc21　　　　98–46812

British Library Cataloguing in Publication Data is available.

Library of Congress Catalog Card Number: 98–46812
ISBN: 0–313–30945–0

First published in 1999

Greenwood Press, 88 Post Road West, Westport, CT 06881
An imprint of Greenwood Publishing Group, Inc.
www.greenwood.com

Printed in the United States of America

The paper used in this book complies with the
Permanent Paper Standard issued by the National
Information Standards Organization (Z39.48–1984).

10 9 8 7 6 5 4 3 2 1

For my wife RANU,

son PRADEEP, and

daughter-in-law DEEPA

CONTENTS

INTRODUCTION

Africa is undergoing a process of socio-economic development, and the implications for human rights remain to be fully explored and managed. A few of the dictionary-type works on African human rights organizations relate mostly to non-African organizations. There is a need for a compendium of information about the status of human rights that takes adequate note of nongovernmental African organizations.[1] This dictionary about human rights advocacy groups within Africa is an attempt to produce a reasonably comprehensive book on ideologies, motives, and activities of open organizations concerned with widespread and much talked about human rights violations in the continent. This dictionary details the work and achievements of various African groups, as well as some prominent and demanding international organizations engaged in highlighting general human rights issues in all of Africa. It records the conflicting interests and diversified deeds that have been generated on the rights issues since the formation of the Organization of African Unity in Addis Ababa, Ethiopia in 1963.

This dictionary does not highlight any particular issue regarding the cultural relativism controversy. The historian Claude E. Welch notes that Third World countries have argued that "human rights as defined in post World War II treaties reflect basic values of Western democratic, industrialized states and hence [are] not truly global."[2] Undeniably, the question of achieving and enforcing universal standards on human rights is still problematic. It is admitted that each tradition has its own internal frame of reference because each tradition derives the validity of its precepts and norms from its own cultural sources. If a cultural tradition relates to other traditions at all, it is likely to do so in a negative way and perhaps even in a hostile way. Many Africans have complained that external human rights groups might not have done justice to indigenous approaches toward rights issues. The presentation of this dictionary does not take any particular issue as ultimate truth.

The rise and fall of the three most brutal tyrants — Jean-Bedel Bokassa of the Central African Republic (1966-79), Fernando Macias Nguema of Equatorial Guinea (1968-79), and Idi Amin of Uganda (1971-79) — severely tarnished the human rights image of Africa. These tyrants aroused a level of external criticism for their sustained abuses of civil and political rights that proved to be damaging to Africa as a whole, and in particular to African criticism of human rights violations in white dominated pre-independent South Africa. The apartheid system in South Africa dialectically engendered a strong human rights movement. Both inside Africa and elsewhere there had been persistent urges to call for the maintenance of civil and political rights. Associations in most parts of Africa have, particularly in the 1980s and 1990s, pleaded for strict enforcement of human rights. The Secretary General of the Organization of African Unity, Salim Salim, approved a declaration in July 1990 that recognized the need to promote popular participation in government and to guarantee human rights. This dictionary is likely to generate more active interest in African human rights issues and organizations.

There is a common normative principle shared by all major cultural traditions that, if construed in an enlightened manner, is capable of sustaining universal standards of human rights. There is the golden rule that one should treat other people as he or she wishes to be treated.[3] Quite simply, human rights are concerned with asserting and protecting human dignity; they are ultimately based on a regard for the intensive worth of the individual. An African scholar writes, "This is an eternal and universal phenomenon, and vital to Nigerians and Malays as to Englishmen and Americans."[4] In short, fundamental civil and political rights refer to the protection of citizens rights against governmental infringements. These rights are supposed to preclude arbitrary governmental intrusion into private affairs of ordinary citizens. This dictionary greatly stresses the indigenous work done by small unknown groups as well as well-publicized and much-respected societies and associations that have tried to prevent governmental violations of social and political rights. In this context I have taken note of some selected Western organizations that have emphasized the universal nature of human rights issues.

SCOPE AND NATURE OF NGOs

I have taken a broad view of nongovernmental organizations (NGOs) in describing their motives and actual work. Formal intergovernmental structures established since World War II to deal with human rights have been active in defining norms but slow to implement them. This gap has created an opportunity for NGOs to take up the work of human rights implementation.[5] In virtually every African country, NGOs have protested against violations of rights such as torture, discrimination against ethnic minorities, and violence against refugees, children, and women. No doubt, there has been an increasingly important role for NGOs in Africa. In fact, NGOs, though weak, have taken up meaningful roles in the sphere of human rights in various parts in Africa. It is true to suggest that "the energy, the vision, the drive, the tenacity of the international movement for human rights today lies predominantly with NGOs."[6] Certainly, there is some controversy over the role of NGOs. One authority argues that a human rights NGO is a private association that devotes significant resources to the promotion and protection of human rights. This kind of association does not seek political power like the political parties. By contrast, the author Lowe Livezey follows an expansive approach to examine the political significance of action for human rights by a wide range of NGOs.[7] In this book, I have taken a broad approach in citing the work of NGOs aince the 1970s that have engaged in exposing human rights abuses, discovery of information of human rights practices, and dissemination of that information in influencing the policies of national governments and the international communities. I have focused mostly on Africa, and to a lesser extent international organizations. The generation of NGOs concerned with human rights, led by Amnesty International, has been concerned with human rights issues in other parts of the world as well as in Africa. Some NGOs have a special African focus although they are based outside of Africa, such as the United States based Human Rights Watch/Africa (formerly Africa Watch).

African human rights NGOs are nationally based, broadly critical of their governments, but organizationally weak. Their efforts to investigate and publish arise from bitter experience, as well as personal commitment of concerned indigenous leaders. Some groups are affiliates of political parties, so bias is bound to creep in.[8] Some focus on campaign activities in a direct confrontational manner, whereas others concentrate on promotional work. Some are democratically organized and others are simply one-person shows.[9] This dictionary presents

NGOs, some of which are presumed by some to be prejudiced, whereas some are regarded as impartial and educative. The basic idea is to present information about African organizations whose ideals we may not share totally.

Human rights concerns in Islamic North Africa are hardly new. For years, organizations such as Amnesty International and the International Commission of Jurists have employed a variety of strategies to call attention to abuses that ranged from political arrests to physical torture in detention. What is innovative about the recent North African groups is their local origins and the measure of self-assertion and implied self-criticism. Thus I have carefully detailed the work of these NGOs in Muslim North Africa as well.

Through the efforts of Africans as well as Westerners, a new concept, the right to economic development, has been advanced as part of human rights. The noted Senegalese jurist Keba M'Baye had earlier articulated the right to development within international forums.[10] Another scholar has recently argued with great conviction that at the local level, human rights must be linked to development activities, and development issues need to be viewed in terms of their human rights implications. There is a need to go beyond the "commando" campaign approach in human rights work, to promotional and empowering social action that ensures that the people themselves can claim and defend their rights. For example, working with rural dwellers to enhance their food security also ought to include issues such as land rights, legal means, security of tenure, and their capacity to defend their rights through existing legal means.[11] The **Banjul Charter on Human and Peoples' Rights,** built upon the Universal Declaration and the International Covenants, added peoples' rights, including rights to development, information, and a healthy environment. International human rights law uses the phrase "economic and social rights" with a considerable degree of consistency to distinguish them from "civil and political rights." There is a growing tendency to see the right to employment, or the right to education, as an adjunct to basic political rights.[12] Human rights issues in this case should be linked directly to practical work with the poor, powerless, ethnic minorities, and vulnerable. This dictionary also includes aspects of socioeconomic rights that are deemed by advocacy groups to be within the sphere of human rights. Obviously, all rights to economic development may not fall under the human rights category. This dictionary takes a diversified approach in presentation.

Traditional human rights discourse has developed without much regard to its effects on women. The historical debate over the importance of first generation (civil and political) rights versus second generation (economic and social) human rights has taken place against a political backdrop that rarely includes women's interests on either side. Critics have argued that western governments and experts, in their presentation of African human rights, have insisted on the primacy of civil and political rights.[13] The United Nations Conference on Women held in Beijing, China in 1995 proclaimed to the satisfaction of all that "human rights are women's rights and women's rights are human rights."

Of course, there are some rights that are specific to women such as a woman's right against forced female genital mutilation (FGM) in parts of Africa. Women in Africa, as in other continents, are being abused through overused and abused customary laws, traditions, social practices, and local norms. In almost every African state, as in many other states in the world, there are discriminatory laws, polygynous relations, child marriages, genital mutilations, and outright violence inflicted by husbands. There also is a visible gap between men and women in terms of political and economic power. The idea that women need to be empowered seems to be the prime argument of some women's organizations in Africa.

Since the 1980s, women's rights have been given priority in the debate on democracy and economic development throughout Africa.[14] There has been a growing realization that women's participation as the majority group is essential to all-around development in the continent. There are "seven sins" of development and one is "development without women," because it is grossly inefficient.[15]

Rather than seeing men as the universal oppressors, women should also be seen as partners in oppression and as having the potential of becoming primary oppressors themselves.[16] Contrary to the argument that violence against women is only personal or cultural, it is in fact socio-political. Violence against women in Africa and elsewhere results from the structural relationships of power, domination, and privilege between men and women in society. Women's human rights issues differ from other human rights issues because structural inequality generates specific obstacles to implementation. No doubt, structural inequality results in the perpetuation of injustice and ignorance despite all efforts to enact and enforce legal rights. For instance, in Kenya, a parliamentary National Assembly consistently refused to enact a long-proposed Marriage and Divorce Act that would give women more rights within the family and divorce cases than they have under customary law.[17] Thus I have included women's rights groups that have diverse and varied agendas for the improvement of women's defense.

To create an alternative culture that is responsive to national needs and women's rights, many associations and groups have been formed in recent years to highlight women's rights in Africa. This dictionary includes the work of groups and sub-groups associated with attempts to enhance women's personal, social, and political rights throughout Africa. However, my attempt here is far from comprehensive.

MEANING OF ADVOCACY

The main thrust of the dictionary is to record the nature of exposures, such as the plight of street children or the suffering of refugees, as seen by advocacy groups. Advocacy is a legal term that means pleading the cause of another. It is dependent on information processing, and yet it goes beyond that in using the information to take up the case of those whose rights are violated. Victims are unable to defend themselves. Advocacy involves taking information about events and converting it into an issue on the public agenda. But this is a process whose outcome is uncertain.[18] Generally stated, my work identifies groups and associations that have stood for universal human rights as spelled out by the Universal Declaration of Human Rights (1948) as well as other regional organizations, which have taken a prominent role in social development in recent years. Specifically, it includes the work of three types of human rights:

1. Civil and political rights that are directly linked to traditional Western political thought.
2. The right to economic development as a distinct human right at the collective level.
3. Human rights including socioeconomic rights, such as women's rights (which gained acceptance in the early 1970s) as well as the rights of ethnic minorities, refugees, and children.

Of course, a clear line of distinction has not been made in this dictionary.

No doubt, many groups and associations working on human rights issues in Africa have been overlooked in this compilation, mainly because of the scarcity of materials. In fact, they have long escaped the attention of scholars. I have tried to describe ideologies, programs, and work of NGOs and activist groups, based mostly in Africa. This human rights dictionary of advocacy groups would suggest that more research is desirable and possible.

This dictionary's goal is to demonstrate the extent of indigenous African interests in forming rights groups and associations that cater to the needs of Africans themselves. It should play a key role in providing a meaningful guide to scholars and policy makers, as well as development agents interested in effectively integrating the African population in general development, in which national governments may not be the enemies of the people.

In sum, this dictionary of advocacy organizations chiefly covers the following areas:

1. African human rights agenda.
2. The current status of human rights in all of Africa.
3. Prime strategies of the human rights groups in the face of political pressure by dictators.

Texts in this dictionary have been arranged alphabetically; the index offers easy reference.

NOTES

1. See, Swedish NGO Foundation of Human Rights, *The Status of Human Rights Organizations in Sub-Saharan Africa* (Stockholm, Sweden: The International Human Rights Internship Program Publication, 1994). A recent book has exposed the nature of debate about "opposing viewpoints" in a wide context. See, David L. Brender et al., *Human Rights: Opposing Viewpoints* (San Diego, CA: Greenhaven Press, 1998).

2. David L. Brender et al., *Human Rights: Opposing Viewpoints* (San Diego, CA: Greenhaven Press, 1998), p. 13.

3. Abdullahi Ahmed An-Naim, *Toward an Islamic Revolution, Civil Liberties, Human Rights, and International Law* (Syracuse: Syracuse University Press, 1990), p. 163.

4. Molefi Kete Asante, cited in Issa G. Shivji, *The Concept of Human Rights in Africa* (London: Council for the Development of Economic and Social Research in Africa [CODESRIA] Books), p. 11.

5. Harold K. Jacobson, *Networks of Independence: International Organization and the Global Political System* (New York: Alfred Knopf, 1984).

6. Lowel W. Livezey, *Nongovernmental Organizations and the Ideas of Human Rights* (Princeton, NJ: The Center for International Studies, 1988), p.19.

7. Laurie S. Wiseberg and Lowel W. Livezey, cited in Eileen McCarthy-Arnolds et al., *Africa, Human Rights, and the Global System* (Westport, CT: Greenwood Press, 1994), pp. 83-84.

8. Claude E. Welch, Jr., *Protecting Human Rights in Africa: Roles and Strategies of Nongovernmental Organizations* (Philadelphia: University of Pennsylvania Press, 1995).

9. Akwasi Aidoo, "Africa: Democracy Without Human Rights?" *Human*

Rights Quarterly 15: (1993), pp. 703-715.

10. Keba M'Baye, "Emergence of the 'Right to Development' as a Human Right in the Context of a New International Economic Order," UNESCO Doc. SS-78/CONF. 630/8. July 16, 1979.

11. Akwasi Aidoo, "Africa: Democracy Without Human Rights?" *Human Rights Quarterly* 15: (1993), pp. 703-715.

12. Philip Alston, "Economic and Social Rights," in Louis Henkin and John Lawrence Hargrove, eds., *Human Rights: An Agenda for the Next Century* (Washington, D.C.: The American Society of International Law, 1994).

13. Marsha A. Freeman and A. S. Fraser, "Women's Human Rights: Making the Theory a Reality," in Louis Henkin and John Lawrence Hargrove, eds., *Human Rights: An Agenda for the Next Century* (Washington, D.C.: The American Society of International Law, 1994).

14. Charlotte Bunch, "Women's Rights as Human Rights: Toward a Re-Vision of Human Rights," *Human Rights Quarterly*, 12: (1990), pp. 486-491.

15. Janice W. Wetzel, *The World of Women: In Pursuit of Human Rights* (New York: New York University Press, 1993).

16. Chandra Talpade Mohanty and An Russo et al., eds., *Third World Women and the Politics of Feminism* (Bloomington: Indiana University Press, 1991).

17. Marsha A. Freeman and Arvonne S. Fraser, "Women's Rights: Making the Theory a Reality" in Louis Henkin and John Lawrence Hargrove (eds.), *Human Rights: An Agenda for the Next Century* (Washington, D.C.: The American Society of International Law, 1994).

18. Harry M. Scoble, "Human Rights Non-Governmental Organizations in Black Africa," in Claude E. Welch, Jr., and Ronald I. Meltzer, eds., *Human Rights and Development in Africa* (Albany: State University of New York Press, 1984).

A

ACTION FOR RURAL DEVELOPMENT AND THE ENVIRONMENT (ADRA). (Angola).

Local human rights monitoring was not encouraged by the Angolan government dominated by the Movement for the Popular Liberation of Angola (MPLA). Some churches and civic organizations were involved in discreet human rights education despite governmental hostility. One such group has been the ADRA, which, with the active support of the Association of European Parliamentarians for Action on Africa (AWEPA) holds workshops on civic education and seminars to increase knowledge of the provisions of the Lusaka Protocols of peace and justice. The ADRA distributes information relating to human rights.

Reference: Human Rights Watch, *World Report 1998* (New York: Human Rights Watch, 1998).

ADALCI. (Niger).

This regional dignity group among the Hausa people in Niger works to raise public awareness about general rights.

Reference: US Department of State, *Country Reports on Human Rights Practices for 1993* (Washington, D.C.: Government Printing Office, 1994).

ADVICE DESK FOR ABUSED WOMEN (ADFAW). (South Africa).

This South African NGO, based in major cities including

Durban, estimates that one in every six women in South Africa is regularly assaulted by her partner and that one in four women is at some time forced to flee threatening domestic situations. The organization claims that police, in keeping with traditional social norms, take the abusing man's word as truth and ignore the abused woman's rights. Fear of social stigma and cruel reprisal from their abusive partners compounds women's reluctance to report abuse. The Africa Desk records cases of mistreatment of women, many of whom are black. Until 1993, abused women could seek to stop abuse through a "peace order," which merely constituted a warning. The Family Violence Act introduced an improved and expedited procedure that made it easier and cheaper for battered women to seek interdict from the Magistrate against an abusive partner. The organization of the Africa Desk stands for women's social as well as general rights.

Reference: Human Rights Watch, *The Human Rights Watch Global Report on Women's Human Rights* (New York: Human Rights Watch, 1995).

ADVICE OFFICES (AO). (South Africa).

Because of the staggering levels of violence in South Africa during the apartheid regimes, South Africans and foreigners created a network of AOs in small towns in rural South Africa. These centers, run mostly by churchmen and largely dependent on private charity, offered a place where people could learn about the law regarding individual rights. The AO offered suggestions about how to seek legal redress of grievances. One clergy, Sheen Duncan, claimed that the abuse of power "is experienced worldwide by the poor people but is exacerbated by South Africa's apartheid laws, by the ongoing state of emergency, and by gross exploitation of unorganized workers by their employers." In August 1989, an AO was opened in an isolated village in Eastern Cape. In February 1989, when workers posted politically provocative posters, the government arrested them and confiscated office equipment. Currently, this organization works in collaboration with the Black Sash group, which has a network of advice offices.

References: Human Rights Watch, *No Neutral Ground: South Africa's Confrontation with Activist Churches* (New York: Human Rights Watch, 1989); US Department of State, *Country Reports on Human Rights*

Practices for 1993 (Washington, D.C.: Government Printing Office, 1994).

AFRICA LEGAL AID (ALA). (Ghana).

This Accra-based NGO was established in 1995. It currently assists other NGOs, individuals, and some regional organizations in preparing complaints to the African Commission. Most complaints of this group state only the facts and refer to the provisions of the African Charter that might have been violated. These complaints generally are not supported by persuasive arguments, namely how the African Charter has been violated, or how the alleged violation of rights has constituted cases of violations. The group has so far provided only legal aid.

Reference: Evelyn A. Ankumah, *The African Commission on Human and Peoples' Rights: Practices and Procedures* (The Hague: Human Rights Commission, 1996).

AFRICA WATCH. (USA).

Africa Watch was established in May 1988 to monitor and promote respect for internationally recognized human rights in Africa. Africa Watch is part of **Human Rights Watch**. Human Rights Watch began in 1978 with the founding of Helsinki Watch by a group of publishers, lawyers, and other activists and now maintains offices in New York, Washington, D.C., London, and elsewhere. Currently, Human Rights Watch has five divisions — Asia Watch, Africa Watch, Americas Watch, Helsinki Watch, and Middle East Watch — all funded by private foundations and individuals. As an NGO, Africa Watch is supported by contributions from private individuals and foundations in the West. Africa Watch, with its headquarters outside the continent, monitors and promotes a variety of human rights abuses in Africa. It reports, among other things, on violations of the laws of war by both governments and insurgent forces. It evaluates these practices by applying standards, to the disagreement of many African leaders, that have been established in international legal instruments, such as the International Covenant on Civil and Political Rights (1966). On April 30, 1991, Africa Watch released a report titled, "Ethiopia: Human Rights Crisis," claiming that the Ethiopian People's Revolutionary

Democratic Front killed a number of people "either directly or indirectly." It reported numerous "killings," "detentions," and "summary executions" in Ethiopia even after the fall of the military dictator Mengistu Haile Mariam. In 1993, Africa Watch published a detailed report about civil and political rights violations in Kenya. The report noted that the government-sponsored ethnic violence in Kenya had resulted in the deaths of over 1,500 people and the displacement of over 300,000. The majority of victims were non-Kalenjins (Kalenjins are President Moi's ethnic groups). Hundreds of youths with bows and arrows systematically attacked ethnic rivals. There appeared to be several motives for the violence. First, it was intended to prove the government's assertion that multi-party politics would lead to tribal chaos. Second, it was intended to punish ethnic groups that were perceived to support the political opposition, namely the Kikuyu, Luhya, and Luo. Third, it was expected to terrorize non-Kalenjins to leave rift valley province, Kenya's most fertile farmland. Currently, Africa Watch relies in most cases on African monitors and informers. Africans have given adequate moral support to the organization. To the dismay of most African dictatorial leaders, Africa Watch has been able to widen its scope of investigations to record abuses of the rights of refugees, children, and minorities.

References: Nigerian Federal Ministry of Justice, *Perspectives on Human Rights* (Lagos, Nigeria: Federal Ministry of Justice, 1992); Africa Watch, *Divide and Rule (Kenya)* (New York: Human Rights Watch, 1993).

AFRICAN ASSOCIATION ON HUMAN AND PEOPLE'S RIGHTS IN DEVELOPMENT (AAHPRID). (Zimbabwe).

Launched in Harare in Zimbabwe, this is a regional cooperative attempt to highlight the need of ordinary citizens for technological and communication opportunities. It arose out of two conferences held in Botswana in 1982 and 1985, which had proposed the creation of a human rights group for development. More than 40 founding members of AAHPRID formally accepted a constitution. The organization exposed the sad conditions in human rights in several countries, including Uganda, Lesotho, and Ghana. One argument was that the absence of any country linked to the African Commission on

Peoples' and Human Rights was a major weakness for the organization. Several presentations by African scholars at the Harare, Zimbabwe, conference focused on women's rights, trade unions, and family law, as well as the problem of judges who were not bold enough to speak out openly about abuses. Several conferences under the auspices of AAHPRID in the 1980s made it clear that ordinary Africans were ready to take steps to enhance human and people's rights. It embraces everything that is current in the human rights discourse on Africa to expose human rights violations in the continent.

References: Claude E. Welch, Jr. (ed.), *Human Rights in Developing Countries: Problems and Prospects: Sub-Saharan Africa*, vol. 1 (Buffalo, New York: State University of New York, 1989); Issa G. Shivji, *The Concept of Human Rights in Africa* (London: CODESRIA Books, 1989).

AFRICAN BAR ASSOCIATION (ABA). (Kenya).

Based in Kenya, this English-speaking legal group encouraged the drafting of a human rights charter for Kenya. It has been active in legal aid, but its activities have largely been confined to questions related to rule of law. It seems to have done very little with regard to the exposition of the human rights violations in Kenya.

Reference: Issa G. Shivji, *The Concept of Human Rights in Africa* (London: CODESRIA, 1989).

AFRICAN BAR ASSOCIATION (ABA). (Zimbabwe).

This regional group addresses the basic principle in regional, national, and international laws relating to the independence of the legal profession and the importance of this principle for the proper administration of justice in the continent. This principle extends to practicing lawyers, defense counsels, academics, human rights activists, and other nongovernmental lawyers. In 1991, the ABA's chairman, Rodger Chongwe of Zambia, argued that the role of lawyers was crucial for the restoration of human rights and for the development of democracy and constitutionalism. According to Chongwe, African lawyers had a role in preventing illegitimate activities, such as military takeovers of constitutional governments, one-party states, and presidencies-for-life, all of which contributed to human rights abuses.

Reference: Raoul Wallenberg Institute, *Human Rights Workshop Namibia* (Lund: The Institute, February 1991).

AFRICAN CENTER FOR DEMOCRACY AND HUMAN RIGHTS STUDIES (ACDHRS). (The Gambia).

This Banjul-based center was organized in 1989 with the support of the **International Commission of Jurists** in Geneva and the government of The Gambia. When the **African Charter on Human and Peoples' Rights** (Banjul Charter) came into force in 1986, The Gambian government pleaded that a center be established to act as a regional NGO that would cooperate closely with the **African Commission on Human and Peoples' Rights**. When the center was established with the financial support of the Banjul government, it was "mandated to encourage the promotion of human and peoples' rights through training and research, in cooperation with other African and international institutions." In the 1980s, it organized several workshops and seminars in rural areas as well as in towns in The Gambia to report cases of rights abuses. This group cited the press that reported that inmates in prisons received inadequate care and nutrition. The ACDHRS found that medical care and hygienic conditions were not satisfactory. For publicity and education, the ACDHRS publishes a newsletter and relevant international human rights materials, organizes regional human rights forums, conducts research on human rights and democracy in Africa, and sustains a training and internship program for participants. The ACDHRS has been active in inspecting prison conditions in The Gambia. The Gambia is also the home to the **Organization of African Unity's** Commission on Human and Peoples' Rights, which is charged to promote and protect human rights in member countries in Africa. There is no other significant local human rights organization in The Gambia.

References: International Commission of Jurists, *Paralegals in Rural Africa* (Geneva, Switzerland: Centre for the Independence of Judges and Lawyers of the International Commission Jurists, 1991); US Department of State, *Country Reports on Human Rights Practices for 1993* (Washington, D.C.: Government Printing Office, 1994).

AFRICAN CENTER FOR INTEGRATED DEVELOPMENT.
(Senegal).

Despite constitutional provision, women in Senegal face enormous discrimination, especially in rural areas where Islamic and Senegalese customs, including polygyny and Islamic rules of inheritance, are strongest. This group is free to criticize the government publicly.

Reference: US Department of State, *Country Reports on Human Rights Practices for 1993* (Washington, D.C.: Government Printing Office, 1994).

AFRICAN CHARTER ON HUMAN AND PEOPLES' RIGHTS
(ACHPR). (The Gambia)

The **Organization of African Unity (OAU)** Heads of States meeting in Nairobi in 1981 adopted the ACHPR, based in Banjul, The Gambia, which came into force in 1986. The phrase "peoples' rights," includes the right to development, which has assumed a central place in human rights resolutions and instruments. The ACHPR emphasized the specificity of African problems relative to human rights. The ACHPR's principles can be divided into three categories:

1. Civil and political rights.
2. Economic, social and cultural rights.
3. Group rights.

But the vagueness of the charter has created problems for its interpretation and uniform application throughout Africa. Despite the emphasis on social, economic, and cultural rights, rights issues are not extensively developed in the charter. In addition, the ACHPR makes only a passing reference to the rights of women. To protect rights enumerated in the ACHPR, the African Commission on Human and Peoples' Rights was created. Since July 1987, the Commission has been charged with the task of dealing with inter-state and "other" communications. The Commission, an organ of the OAU, focuses on specific competencies in the field of human rights. The Commission's report, "stating the facts and its findings," may be made public, but only with the approval of the OAU Assembly. The ACHPR makes it clear that the Commission plays a minor role in enforcement. In fact, the Commission has an ambiguous relationship with the OAU Secretariat in Addis Ababa. No continent-wide court of human rights exists in Africa and as such the Commission has no right to bring cases to any court. It can bring cases of abuses to the attention of the Heads of Assembly of the OAU, but the likelihood of reprisals against individuals often means that victims of abuses usually do not file complaints directly. Individuals also lack the legal and monetary resources necessary to represent their complaints in the manner required by the African Commission. It is not clear whether an individual petition will be considered only when a serious pattern of violation is established. What constitutes a series of "serious or massive" violations needs to be defined. The final verdict on any violation of civil rights lies with the Heads of States. Many are of the opinion that the African Commission should be given the mandate to make final binding decisions. Specific remedies are neither provided for, nor does the ACHPR spell out how the recommendations should be implemented. By the end of 1994, the Commission received 35 individual complaints, but their nature and extent were kept confidential. Some NGOs have recently been given observer status by the Commission to monitor human rights violations.

References: Harry M. Scoble, "Human Rights Non-Governmental Organizations in Black Africa" in Claude E. Welch, Jr., and R. I. Meltzer (eds.), *Human Rights and Development in Africa* (Albany: State University of New York Press, 1984); N.S. Rembe, *The System of Protection of Human Rights Under the African Charter on Human and Peoples' Rights* (Rome: Human Rights Groups, 1991).

AFRICAN COMMISSION OF HEALTH AND HUMAN RIGHTS PROMOTERS (ACHHRP). (Ghana).

This NGO, established in 1992, operates clinics in Ghana that provide free medical assistance and counseling to women suffering from domestic abuses and other problems. Dr. Edmund Delle, the director of the group, notes that in many parts of Ghana, female genital mutilations had been practiced regularly. He believes that domestic violence is still widespread. The ACHHRP runs a shelter in Accra to provide temporary shelter for sufferers.

Reference: Human Rights Internet, *Ghana: Update on the Fourth Republic* (Ottawa, Canada: University of Ottawa Press, 1994).

AFRICAN COMMITTEE FOR LAW AND DEVELOPMENT (CADD). (Senegal).

This regional group of West African states was established in 1990, but it became operational in 1992. CADD was created as an international organization with branches in countries such as Benin, Mali, Nigeria, and Senegal. It wanted to promote and protect human rights and incorporate the rule of law in democratic and development processes in Africa. It has an executive committee of seven members.

Reference: Swedish NGO Foundation for Human Rights, *The Status of Human Rights Organizations in Sub-Saharan Africa* (Stockholm: The International Human Rights Internship Program Publications, 1994).

AFRICAN FEDERATION OF WOMEN OF SENEGAL. (Senegal).

This NGO defends women's rights in general. There is much discrimination against women in educational opportunities; they receive less than one-third of the schooling received by men. Although family laws have been passed to give more rights to women in divorce cases and other matters, laws are rarely enforced. There are reports that wife beating is common.

Reference: US Department of State, *Country Reports on Human Rights Practices for 1993* (Washington, D.C.: Government Printing Office, 1994).

AFRICAN HUMAN RIGHTS AND JUSTICE PROTECTION NETWORK. (Tanzania).

The Tanzanian government has generally obstructed the formation of local human rights groups. The Network complains that its work to get access and monitor human rights violations has been hampered because the government will not register the group. The government claims that the group has political motives.

Reference: US Department of State, *Country Reports on Human Rights Practices for 1993* (Washington, D.C.: Government Printing Office, 1994).

AFRICAN NETWORK FOR THE PREVENTION AND PROTECTION AGAINST CHILD ABUSE AND NEGLECT (ANPPCAN). (Kenya).

The Kenyan branch of ANPPCAN, an NGO, brings criminal

action against the Kenyan police. It is a legal advocacy group on behalf of the arrested children in Kenya. In one instance, it protested the shooting and killing of a child, Kajunia, arguing that the lethal use of force against him was totally unwarranted. The branch started a legal defense unit to provide legal assistance and representation to children, including street children.

Reference: Human Rights Watch, *Juvenile Injustice: Police Abuse and Detention of Street Children in Kenya* (New York: Human Rights Watch, 1997).

AGISANANG DOMESTIC ABUSE PREVENTION AND TRAINING (ADAPT). (South Africa).

This NGO, with an office at Alexandra, has made a number of significant efforts to address the state's inadequate response to domestic violence and rape. The organization argues that as long as the police and judicial systems are seen as failing to bring criminals to justice, people in the townships will continue to take the law into their hands. It feels that vigilante justice is arbitrary and reinforces a cycle of violence.

Reference: Human Rights Watch, *Violence Against Women in South Africa* (New York: Human Rights Watch, 1995).

ALGERIAN LEAGUE FOR HUMAN RIGHTS (LADH). (Algeria).

There are two leagues — one recognized by the Algerian government and one affiliated with the Paris-based International Federation of Human Rights. Both began in the mid-1980s to denounce government human rights abuses. The LADH, which is associated with Paris-based human rights groups, has been active in recording political and civil rights violations in Algeria. At times it works in consultation with Abdennour Ali-Yahia, an outspoken critic of the government, and the president of the **Algerian League for the Defense of Human Rights**. Ali-Yahia has for long been associated with a Berber movement of cultural separatism. The LADH and other human rights groups in Algeria have campaigned for the protection and extension of women's rights since the 1990 Islamist victory in municipal elections. Of the two national leagues, the LADH is less outspoken. The state of siege decree of June 4, 1991, gave the military the power to perform police functions and conduct trials of civilian suspects. The LADH claimed that 8,000 civilians were arrested under this decree. When a legislative decree was made public in October 1992, for suppression of so-called "terrorism," the LADH called the decree fundamentally "reprehensible." It argued that the provisions of the decree of 1992 posed a serious threat to human rights.

References: Susan Waltz, "Making Waves: The Political Impact of Human Rights Groups in North Africa," *Journal of Modern African Studies*, 29, 3: (1991), 481-504; Middle East Watch, *Human Rights Abuses in Algeria: No One Is Spared* (New York: Human Rights Watch, 1994).

ALGERIAN LEAGUE FOR THE DEFENSE OF HUMAN RIGHTS (LADDH). (Algeria).

The LADDH is one of the two national human rights organizations in Algeria. Its president in 1992 was Abdennour Ali-Yahia, an outspoken critic of the military government's Legislative Decree 92-03 (September 1992) relative to the struggle against subversion and terrorism. Ali claimed that the decree violated the constitution as well as the conventions and international pacts that Algeria had ratified. His concern was that the military decree was too broad and that it unjustifiably included a variety of nonviolent actions, including speech and association.

Reference: Middle East Watch, *Human Rights Abuses in Algeria* (New York: Human Rights Watch, 1994).

ALL WOMEN'S ASSOCIATION OF GHANA (AWAG). (Ghana).

Women in Ghana manage this emerging human rights association, which is concerned with women's social issues. Its members have not consciously identified themselves as feminists, but they are concerned with hardships caused by women's genital operations, traditional widowhood, and inheritance laws. The association's attempts are integral aspects of the international movement to establish and protect human rights, especially the rights of women.

Reference: George W. Shepherd, Jr. and Mark O. Anikpo (eds.), *Emerging Human Rights* (Westport, CT: Greenwood Press, 1990).

AMNESTY INTERNATIONAL (AI). (England).

This London-based international NGO was founded in 1961. It

has become a highly respectable organization and has been faithfully reporting gross violations of human rights all over the world. In 1977, it was awarded the Nobel Prize for Peace. AI's African dimension is significant. It reports on the treatment of political prisoners, political torture, and the death penalty in Africa. It gave extensive coverage to the "Red Terror" of 1976-1978 in Ethiopia in which the Derg (a Marxist-Leninist military committee in Ethiopia, 1974-1991) ruthlessly crushed rival leftist movements. Under decrees issued by the Derg in November 1974, military tribunals were established with powers to impose death penalties for political offenses in Ethiopia. AI, a giant among human rights groups, campaigned against these decrees. Through the 1980s, AI addressed issues of political prisoners, torture, disappearances, extra-judicial executions, and killings of civilians in the areas of armed conflicts, particularly in Eritrea. AI helps "prisoners of conscience" — persons imprisoned for peacefully exercising their basic human rights. For instance, it wrote to Nigerian authorities requesting that incarcerated Nigerian journalists be released. The organization's researchers treated information from politically partisan sources with caution.

References: Eileen McCarthy-Arnolds et al., *Africa, Human Rights, and the Global System* (Westport, CT: Greenwood Press, 1994), 83-84; Amnesty International, *Human Rights Violations in Ethiopia* (London: Amnesty International, 1978).

AMOS GROUP. (Democratic Republic of Congo, formerly Zaire).
This small NGO is concerned with political repression. It made little progress during the Mobutu regime in Zaire.

Reference: US Department of State, *Country Reports on Human Rights Practices for 1993* (Washington, D.C.: Government Printing Office, 1994).

ANGOLAN CAMPAIGN TO BAN LANDMINES (CABM).
(Angola).
This private group was launched in November 1996 to publicize the idea that antipersonnel mines were abuses of human rights. It actively and increasingly campaigned against landmines in Angola and collected 60,000 signatures from the public in a petition asking for a total ban. For public awareness, the CABM organized exhibitions in Kuito,

Malange, and Lubango. It was also active in lobbying Angolan National Assembly members. The government was supportive of the call.

Reference: Human Rights Watch, *World Report 1998* (New York: Human Rights Watch, 1998).

ANGOLAN HUMAN RIGHTS ASSOCIATION (AADH). (Angola).
This is one of the two main national human rights groups in Angola where the central government has been dominated by the MPLA party. This Luanda-based NGO is the largest human rights group in Angola. Because the UNITA party controlled most of Angola's territory, the Angolan central government had little influence on investigations of human rights abuses in most parts of the country. Even today prison conditions remain very bad. The association, which visited prisons in the Luanda area, reported appalling conditions. It reported that of the 1,513 inmates in 1995, only 175 had been charged formally. One objective of this organization is to distribute information about prison conditions in Angola.

References: Human Rights Watch, *Angola* (New York: Human Rights Watch, 1996); US Department of State, *Country Reports on Human Rights Practices for 1993* (Washington, D.C.: Government Printing Office, 1994).

ANGOLAN HUMAN RIGHTS NUCLEUS (AHRN). (Angola).
The AHRN is one of two national groups concerned with human rights investigations. Because the UNITA party controlled most of Angola's national territory, the central government could do little to investigate cases of human rights abuses. UNITA did not allow NGOs any access to territories under its control because of political rivalry and competing claims. Despite elections, central governmental power remained in the hands of a small MPLA elite. AHRN Investigations of human rights abuses remained minimal in 1993 because of a shortage of funds as well as a lack of good leadership. However, a newly established Human Rights Sub-Committee in the MPLA-dominated Parliament became somewhat active. The Sub-Committee published reports critical of the government, observing that there were laws to protect human rights but no mechanism to enforce the laws.

Reference: US Department of State, *Country Reports on Human Rights*

Practices for 1993 (Washington, D.C.: Government Printing Office, 1994).

ARAB INSTITUTE FOR HUMAN RIGHTS. (Algeria).

The General Assembly of a few African countries elected a board of trustees consisting of 15 members who were to meet annually to discuss human rights issues. With the support of this group and in line with the recommendations of the UN Charter for Human Rights, the Arab Institute for Human Rights was set up in Tunis to provide information on human rights conditions and training for both government and nongovernmental personnel.

Reference: Jack Donnelly, *International Human Rights* (Boulder, CO: Westview Press, 1993).

ARAB LAWYERS' UNION. (Egypt).

Founded in 1958, the Arab Lawyers Union has been working to facilitate contacts between Arab lawyers, to assure the freedom of lawyers in their work and the independence of magistrates, and to allow all Arab lawyers to take cases in any Arab country. The union was instrumental in founding an **Arab Organization for Human Rights**. Generally, the Sudanese government keeps political dissidents in detention centers in Khartoum known as "ghost houses," where detainees are beaten upon arrival and tortured during interrogation. They are released without charge several days later. According to the Union, such brief periods of detention and torture without charge, ranging from two weeks to as long as six months, are increasingly common tactics used by the ruling National Salvation Revolutionary Command Council in Sudan to harass perceived critics and political opponents.

References: Edward Lawson, *Encyclopedia of Human Rights* (New York: Taylor and Francis, 1991); Lawyers Committee for Human Rights, *In Defense of Rights: Attacks on Lawyers and Judges in 1993* (New York: Lawyers Committee for Human Rights, 1993).

ARAB LEAGUE FOR HUMAN RIGHTS (ALHR). (Algeria).

One of ALHR's main objectives was to bring about the civil society, which "has been absorbed by the state and the single party." The ALHR claimed that the Algerian government was responsible for the adverse and unhealthy social, political, and moral conditions that led to popular disturbances in the late 1980s.

Reference: Human Rights Internet, *Human Rights Internet: Reporter* (Boston, MA: Harvard Law School, February 1994).

ARAB ORGANIZATION FOR HUMAN RIGHTS (AOHR).
(Egypt).

This Giza-based organization was originally founded in December 1983 in Cyprus, when statutes were adopted, following resolutions in a meeting held in April 1983 in Tunis. The AOHR called for respect of human rights and fundamental freedom of all citizens and residents of the Arab world. Now it defends any individual whose human rights are subjected to violations that are contrary to the Universal Declaration of Human Rights. It provides legal assistance where necessary and possible, and calls for improvements in conditions of prisoners of conscience. Above all, it coordinates efforts with the **Arab Lawyers Union.** Thus keeps the human rights idea alive at least on the fringes of the political debate in some countries in Africa.

References: Jack Donnelly, *International Human Rights* (Boulder, CO: Westview Press, 1993); Arab Organization For Human Rights, "Human Rights," Giza, Egypt: http://192.203.180.62/mlas /aohr.htm

ARAB WOMEN'S SOLIDARITY ASSOCIATION (AWSA).
(Egypt).

This Cairo-based Muslim women's association headed by Nawal al-Saadawi, an internationally known writer and leader in Egyptian women's affairs. This liberal association of educated women had a history of tense relations with the Egyptian authorities. Nevertheless, it had obtained permission from the Social Affairs Ministry for its operation in January 1983. The AWSA has consultative status as an NGO with the UN Economic and Social Council. For some time it operated with the tacit approval of the Egyptian Foreign Ministry. But on June 15, 1991, the Deputy Governor of Cairo, without any prior warning, issued an administrative decree dissolving the AWSA. The apparent ease with which the Egyptian authorities have been able to replace an outspoken independent organization provides a clear example of the extensive power of the Egyptian government to control the activities of the nongovernmental human rights organizations.

Reference: EOHR, *Lawyers Committee for Human Rights: North Africa* (Giza, Egypt: Lawyers Committee for Human Rights, 1991).

ASSOCIATION FOR THE DEFENSE OF HUMAN RIGHTS (AZADHO). (Democratic Republic of Congo, formerly Zaire).

People in Shaba province believed that the rough and tough Katangese youth bands, functioned with the support of the central administration. The attacking youths were recruited from villages across Katanga and trained at locations in small towns. The violence against Kasaiens affected the lives of thousands of people, although the government argued that the protesters could be identified with the political opposition. The AZADHO complained that the perpetrators of violence against citizens in Shaba province were protected by the Mobutu government. Many atrocities against Kasaiens have been recorded by the AZADHO.

Reference: Africa Watch, *Zaire: Inciting Hatred: Violence Against Kasaiens in Shaba* (New York: Human Rights Watch, 1993).

ASSOCIATION FOR THE DEFENCE OF HUMAN RIGHTS (ADDH). (Mozambique).

There are several human rights concerns in Mozambique, including the restrictions on freedom of expression the movement of the former armed opposition, and the sad conditions in prisons. The ADDH visited some prisons in Maputo in 1997 and wrote several letters to the press.

Reference: Human Rights Watch, *World Report 1998* (New York: Human Rights Watch, 1998).

ASSOCIATION FOR THE DEFENSE OF HUMAN RIGHTS AND LIBERTIES (ADDHL). (Djibouti).

Since independence in 1977, Djibouti remained a de facto one-party state. In 1993, President Hassan Gouled Aptidon and his party, the People's Rally, controlled virtually all aspects of civil and political life. The Afars comprise the largest tribe, but they are outnumbered by the Issa (the tribe of the President) and other Somali clans taken together. The government's virtual military occupation of the north led to the abuse of the Afar civilians living there. Violence against women and children was not uncommon. The government refused to recognize the ADDHL. In 1996, the ADDHL publicly stopped criticizing the government, which continued to deny this rights group any recognition. This NGO reports on killings and other human rights violations by the army. It claimed that political prisoners are prisoners of conscience, having committed no crimes. It claimed that innocent Afa civilians were often killed by the government and para-military forces in northern Djibouti. In one case, soldiers killed a father and a son, Mola Omar and Muhammad Mola, near the town of Lahassa. International organizations and independent observers also reported killings of civilians. Of course, the government denied that there had been any mass killings by soldiers. Its president in 1993 was Mohamed Houmed Soulleh. In June 1993, the government refused to grant travel documents to the President of Djiboutian Association for the Respect of Human Rights and Liberties who had hoped to attend the Vienna International Conference on Human Rights.

References: US Department of State, *Country Reports of Human Rights Practices for 1993* (Washington, D.C.: Government Printing Office, 1994); Amnesty International USA, *Amnesty International Report* (New York: Amnesty International Publications, 1994).

ASSOCIATION FOR THE PROMOTION OF THE RULE OF LAW. (Togo).

Several private human rights groups exist in Togo. Among them are **Togolese League of Human Rights** and the Association for the Promotion of the Rule of Law. But these two are not able to perform effectively. President G. Eyadema did not allow the human rights organizations to do any monitoring. The **National Human Rights Commission (CNDH)**, established by the government, also was largely inactive.

Reference: US Department of State, *Country Reports on Human Rights Practices for 1993* (Washington, D.C.: Government Printing Office, 1994).

ASSOCIATION FOR WIDOWS OF THE APRIL GENOCIDE (AVEGA). (Rwanda).

During the 1994 genocide, Rwandan women were subjected to sexual violence on a massive scale, perpetuated by members of the infamous Hutu militia groups, by civilians, and by soldiers. The group's leading spokesperson is Annuciate Nyiratamba. Many women survivors are angry that the abuses against them are not being adequately addressed. Thus A. Nyiratamba claimed in 1996 that women were alone, and no one spoke about the survivors. This organization now organizes and empowers women, but the Rwandan authorities are not very supportive of the efforts.

Reference: Human Rights Watch, *Shattered Lives: Rwandan Genocide* (New York: Human Rights Watch, 1996).

ASSOCIATION OF CHRISTIANS AGAINST TORTURE (ACAT). (Benin).

The Republic of Benin had a constitutional government headed by President Nicephore Soglo, elected in 1991. This NGO's activities included drawing attention to poor prison conditions. It was dissatisfied with the procedural delays in most court cases. The current government, however, has welcomed nongovernmental scrutiny of human rights in Benin.

Reference: US Department of State, *Country Reports on Human Rights Practices for 1993* (Washington, D.C.: Government Printing Office, 1994).

ASSOCIATION OF HANDICAPPED MILITARY AND PARAMILITARY MOZAMBICANS (ADEMINO). (Mozambique).

This group represents disabled demobilized soldiers. This is smaller than the **Association of Mozambican Disabled (ADEMO).** It attempts to raise public awareness of the need to integrate the disabled into society, and asks the government to initiate legislation to support the working rights of the disabled. In 1996, the ADEMINO charged that the Mozambican government had not yet authorized medical pensions for the disabled soldiers.

Reference: US Department of State, *Country Reports on Human Rights Practices for 1993* (Washington, D.C.: Government Printing Office, 1994).

ASSOCIATION OF HUMAN RIGHTS PROMOTERS (ASHURIP). (Liberia).

Based in Monrovia and founded by a former government

employee in 1991, this small private organization focuses on human rights education in Liberia. With 300 members, the group works sometimes in collaboration with the Catholic Justice and Peace Commission to promote human rights. Lack of funds has rendered the organization ineffective in civil war torn Liberia.

Reference: Human Rights Library, University of Minnesota, "Human Rights," http://www.umn.edu/humanrts/africa/liberia.htm

ASSOCIATION OF IVORIAN WOMEN (AFI). (Ivory Coast).

During the 1960s, the government of Houphouet-Boigny established a husband's right to control much of his wife's property. To open a bank account or to obtain a job, women in the Ivory Coast had to seek their husbands' permission. The AFI reacted to establish women's rights in personal spheres. At its insistence, the government was obliged to accept in 1976 the AFI leader Jeanne Gervais as government minister to look after women's interests. Her primary goal was to obtain judicial equality for women. Yet in reality the status of women remained below the status of men in the Ivory Coast throughout the 1980s.

Reference: Robert E. Handloff (ed.), *Cote d'Ivoire: A Country Study* (Washington, D.C.: Government Printing Office, 1988).

ASSOCIATION OF LAW SOCIETIES (ALS). (South Africa).

This association works for law-related education programs, to be taught to South African school children. Its Street Law Program attempts to make students aware that even political detainees have legal rights and that the court will protect them from unlawful treatment. It teaches that if detainees are being assaulted by the police, their relatives may obtain a court order to prevent such assaults. Under the auspices of the ALS, an informative program teaches students that the powers of the police to arrest a person are carefully controlled by the law. This association has developed the first fully-fledged program at the University of Natal, Durban in 1987. The program has since spread to ten other universities in South Africa. By the end of 1992, the Street Law program, which was largely funded by American private donors, was taught to school children in 2,000 schools. The varied programs make people on the street aware of their rights, and encourage them to think about the type of legal system that they would like to have in new South Africa. The detailed program deals with the protection of human rights in criminal justice proceedings with respect to:

- powers of the police to arrest
- detention without trial
- searches and seizures
- criminal trials
- the sentencing process
- juvenile justice.

Reference: M. Cheri Bassiouni and Ziyad Motala (eds.), *The Protection of Human Rights in African Criminal Proceedings* (London: Martinus Publishers, 1995).

ASSOCIATION OF MAURITANIANS IN SENEGAL. (Senegal).

This group defends the cause of the refugees who have been forced to flee by the action of the Mauritanian military government in the late 1980s. In Banjul, the association met the representatives of the **International Commission of Jurists** to discuss human rights issues, especially rights of the refugees residing in Senegal. But the Mauritanian government refused to allow the International Commission of Jurists to visit Mauritania. The government claimed that it put no restrictions on the return of those who were expelled during 1989-90, including the Senegalese previously resident in Mauritania.

Reference: US Department of State, *Country Reports on Human Rights Practices for 1993* (Washington, D.C.: Government Printing Office, 1994).

ASSOCIATION OF MOZAMBICAN DISABLED (ADEMO).
(Mozambique).

This group represents children and women who suffer variously in this civil war torn country. According to medical and other sources, violence against women is frequent; wife beating is common. Cases relating to women are rarely brought to courts. Likewise, children's rights and welfare have not been a priority of the Mozambican government in the past and at present. Children who were taken from their homes during the civil war have yet to be reunited with their families. The ADEMO was established to plead for legal rights of these disadvantaged groups.

Reference: US Department of State, *Country Reports on Human Rights Practices for 1993* (Washington, D.C.: Government Printing Office, 1994).

ASSOCIATION OF VICTIMS OF REPRESSION (AVR). (Guinea).
In Guinea there were no reports of political killings in the early 1980s, but there were a number of extrajudicial killings. Security forces used excessive force in responding to political demonstrations. Human rights remained circumscribed despite holding presidential elections. There was no progress in resolving the disappearances of 63 people arrested in the wake of the April 1984 seizure of power and the July 1985 coup attempt. In 1992, the AVR filed a legal suit against government officials involved in the arrests. This group has been vocal in calling attention to human rights abuses in Guinea but has to be cautious in criticizing the government.

Reference: US Department of State, *Country Reports on Human Rights Practices for 1993* (Washington, D.C.: Government Printing Office, 1994).

ASSOCIATION OF WOMEN AGAINST VIOLENCE. (Cameroon).
Women suffer from various discriminations. There is the social problem of female genital mutilation, although the government does not recognize this as a social problem. This women's group is concerned with the raising of public awareness about the plight of women. This group works mostly through publicity.

Reference: US Department of State, *Country Reports on Human Rights Practices for 1993* (Washington, D.C.: Government Printing Office, 1994).

ASSOCIATION OF WOMEN JURISTS. (Chad).
Domestic violence directed against women is common, and women have only limited legal recourses against abusive spouses. This association was instrumental in pressing for improvements in women's rights at the National Conference in 1993 (Washington, D.C.: Government Printing Office, 1994).

Reference: US State Department, *Country Report on Human Rights*

Practices for 1993 (Washington, D.C.: Government Printing Office, 1994).

ASSOCIATION OF WOMEN MERCHANTS (of Kisangani) (Association des Femmes Commerscantees). (Democratic Republic of Congo, formerly Zaire).

> This Zairian women's body is engaged in preserving trading interests of market women. Gradually, the group has turned into a vehicle for class interests. It argues that it is a case of victory of class solidarity over gender solidarity.

References: Sandra W. Meditz (ed.), *Zaire: A Country Study* (Washington, D.C.: Government Printing Office, 1993); Janet MacGaffey (ed.), *The Real Economy of Zaire: The Contribution of Smuggling and Other Unofficial Activities to National Wealth* (Philadelphia: University of Pennsylvania Press, 1991).

ASSOCIATION OF WOMEN, LAW, AND DEVELOPMENT (MULEIDE). (Mozambique).

> This association was established to safeguard the legal rights of women and children. Its activities have so far been limited.

Reference: US Department of State, *Country Reports on Human Rights Practices for 1993* (Washington, D.C.: Government Printing Office, 1994).

ASSOCIATION OF YOUNG SENEGALESE LAWYERS (AJAS). (Senegal).

> The AJAS has carried out "legal tours" of some regions of Senegal to spread the idea of legal rights. During the tours, the organization used the radio to spread information on human rights of ordinary people. Currently, it provides free legal consultation and arranges prison visits. It has taken some cases of pretrial detainees to court.

Reference: Swedish NGO Foundation for Human Rights, *The Status of Human Rights Organizations in Sub-Saharan Africa* (Stockholm: The International Human Rights Internship Program Publications, 1994).

AUMONERIE CATHOLIQUE. (Madagascar).

> In 1996, more than 70 percent of the estimated persons in custody were in pretrial detention. The accused very often remained in police custody for years only to be exonerated in court. This Catholic NGO, in partnership with the Young

Lawyers' Association, pursued case reviews of a number of detainees in Madagascar.

Reference: US Department of State, *Country Reports on Human Rights Practices for 1993* (Washington, D.C.: Government Printing Office, 1994).

AVOCATS SANS FRONTIERES. (Rwanda).

The government of Rwanda acknowledged the rights of the accused to legal defense, but declared itself unable to pay for legal assistance. Avocats, a small NGO, arranged for attorneys from other African countries to represent some defendants, but it lacked the resources to meet the growing demand. Currently, their staff can not provide assistance in insecure areas.

Reference: Human Rights Watch, *World Report 1998* (New York: Human Rights Watch, 1998).

B

BANJUL CHARTER (African Charter on Human and Peoples' Rights). (The Gambia).

One of the reform efforts of the OAU was the African Charter of Human and Peoples' Rights, proposed by President Jawara of the Gambia. The Charter was adopted by the Heads of States of the OAU in Nairobi, Kenya in June 1981; it entered into force on October 21, 1986. The Charter provided for the establishment of a Commission whose members were elected. Although established within the context of the OAU, the Commission is an independent organ. Its "promotion" of rights, involved steps to bolster awareness of human rights, their "protection" meant acting directly on behalf of individuals whose rights were abridged. The Banjul Charter authorized the Commission to receive communications from individuals, as well as from states, but left obscure what it should do with periodic reports from governments. Reports from Libya, Rwanda, and Tunisia were considered in 1991. The reports were brief and without any precise texts. The Commission "lacked adequate equipment, resources and support to make it truly operational." Yet the Banjul Charter is expected to show that African states cannot contract out of international customary law of respect for human rights. The Banjul Charter gives unusual emphasis to collective or people's rights and individual duties (Articles 19-24; 27-29). In sum, the peoples' rights or the collective rights are implicitly subject to interpretation by the government of the state concerned as the custodian of the rights of its people. State rights would take precedence over the rights of individuals. The Charter is not legally enforceable.

References: U. O. Umozurike, *Self-Determination in International Law* (Hamden, CT: Archon, 1972); U. O. Umozurike, "The Protection of Human Rights Under the Banjul African Charter on Human and Peoples' Rights," *African Journal of International Law* 1 (1988), 65-83; Christopher Clapman, *Africa and the International System* (Cambridge, England: Cambridge University Press, 1996).

BATTERED WOMEN'S ACTION GROUP (BWAG). (South Africa).

The BWAG is a coordinating body for abused women. Founded in 1984, it includes health, religious, welfare, and community organizations. It meets regularly to educate each other about battering and to share information with other related organizations. The BWAG serves as a back up to **Rape Crisis**. Its members offer services to battered women, aiding them with a phone-in weekend. The members have launched their counseling services to raise funds and negotiate for a shelter for battered women to be managed by Rape Crisis.

Reference: Janice Wood Wetzel, *The World of Women: In Pursuit of Human Rights* (New York: New York University Press, 1993).

BERBER CULTURAL MOVEMENT (MCB). (Algeria).

Although Algeria's indigenous people, the Berbers, were Arabized to a certain extent, they have maintained their cultural identity, partly through the creation of the MCB in the 1970s. Armed Islamists (GIA) abducted many Berber leaders in 1994. Sporadic Islamist incursions into Kabylia, the Berber region in the north, have been regarded by Berbers as human rights violations. The Algerian government, of course, has been fighting armed Islamist groups. The government also has been blamed for rights violations.

Reference: Human Rights Internet, *Algeria: Islamism, The State and Armed Conflict* (Ottawa: University of Ottawa Press, 1995).

BLACK LAWYERS ASSOCIATION (BLA). (South Africa).

This is an old association for rights. In 1979, a black law clerk was denied admission to the Law Society on grounds of his citizenship in Bophuthatswana. The black lawyers in-group brought a case against the government and won. Gradually the BLA began to concentrate on human rights issues and economic matters.

Reference: Human Rights Internet, *Human Rights Internet: Reporter* (Boston, MA: Harvard Law School, February 1994).

BLACK ROBES (Toges Noire). (Democratic Republic of Congo, formerly Zaire).

This human rights organization is made up of Zairian magistrates and lawyers. It inspects conditions in prisons and police lockups.

Reference: Lawyers Committee for Human Rights, *In Defense of Rights: Attacks on Lawyers and Judges in 1993* (New York: Lawyers Committee for Human Rights, 1993).

BLACK SASH. (South Africa).

This private organization, founded in 1955, now based in Cape Town and having eight other branches, became expert in navigating the varied apartheid issues and laws that governed the black people in South Africa before the African National Congress (ANC) came to power. The Black Sash started its protest program as well as a plan to educate the people on human rights. Bishop Desmond Tutu was instrumental in developing this program which gained momentum after other secular organizations and the churches became involved in rights issues. The Black Sash and several Advice Offices made the public aware of the legal rights and the possibilities of due legal process as a way to solve problems of police harassment. Poor people were informed to tell that in the past "people's basic rights" were being ignored. *Sash* is the publication of this nonpolitical, nonviolent and nondenominational rights group. The specific objectives of the Black Sash are to bring justice to all, to seek constitutional recognition and protection by law of human rights and liberties for all, and to protest race-based housing. The Black Sash maintains "Working Groups" in rural areas; it upholds children's rights as well. It has noted that the majority of domestic violence survivors have not sought official help, but have so far relied on an informal network of family and friends. Indifference toward domestic violence on the part of police, combined with the distrust of the police carried over from the apartheid era, have made women, particularly black women, victims of violence. The Black Sash defends these disadvantaged social groups.

References: Human Rights Watch, *The Human Rights Watch Global Report on Women's Human Rights* (New York: Human Rights Watch, 1998); Human Rights Watch, *No Neutral Ground: South Africa's Confrontation with the Activist Churches* (New York: Human Rights Watch, 1989).

BOTSWANA ASSOCIATION FOR HUMAN RIGHTS (BAHR).
(Botswana).

Botswana is a multi-party democracy and its President, Ketumile Masire, welcomes human rights observers. Local human rights groups operate openly and independently. The BAHR has attempted to get needed legal reforms, to heighten public awareness about human rights, and above all to pressure the government to accept more of the international human rights instruments.

Reference: US Department of State, *Country Reports on Human Rights Practices for 1993* (Washington, D.C.: Government Printing Office, 1994).

BOTSWANA CENTER FOR HUMAN RIGHTS. (Botswana).

In Botswana, there is no public defender service to help needy victims. This right group provides legal aid to the indigent.

Reference: US Department of State, *Country Reports on Human Rights Practices for 1993* (Washington, D.C.: Government Printing Office, 1994).

BURKINABE MOVEMENT FOR HUMAN RIGHTS AND PEOPLES (MBDHP). (Burkina Faso).

President Blaise Compaore dominates the government in this secular state. But during and after general elections in 1991, many opposition leaders and human rights activists were detained. Minorities have been discriminated against. The MBDHP, an independent group composed mostly of professionals and led by magistrates, advocated the release of opposition supporters detained in 1991. The government released these prisoners, but ignored the demands that it should account for the disappearances of Boukary and

Guillaume Sessouma, two prominent leaders.

Reference: US Department of State, *Country Reports on Human Rights Practices for 1993* (Washington, D.C.: Government Printing Office).

BURUNDIAN ASSOCIATION FOR THE DEFENSE OF THE RIGHTS OF PRISONERS. (Burundi).

Local human rights organizations remained constrained in operations in Burundi. The association began a program of monitoring the treatment of the growing prison population. The group had difficulty in receiving authorization to enter prisons and to speak with prisoners.

Reference: Human Rights Watch, *World Report 1998* (New York: Human Rights Watch, 1998).

C

CAMEROON BAR ASSOCIATION. (Cameroon).

This bar association has been active in protesting arrests and detention of political opponents. In March 1990, Bernard Muna, head of the association, criticized human rights violations in Cameroon and called on the bar association to defend political and civil rights.

Reference: Human Rights Watch, *The Persecution of Human Rights Monitors* (New York: Human Rights Watch, 1990).

CAMEROON HUMAN RIGHTS LEAGUE. (France).

This nongovernmental human rights organization based in France is concerned with political and civil rights violations in Cameroon. It argues that many opponents of the government are being held without trial.

Reference: Amnesty International USA, *Amnesty International Report 1994* (New York: Amnesty International Publications, 1994).

CAMEROONIAN ASSOCIATION FOR CHILDREN'S RIGHTS. (Cameroon).

Babies and small children are sometimes held in prison if their mothers are incarcerated. This NGO is concerned with child welfare and the inappropriate treatment of children.

Reference: US Department of State, *Country Reports of Human Rights Practices for 1993* (Washington, D.C.: Government Printing Office, 1997).

CAMEROONIAN ASSOCIATION OF FEMALE JURISTS.
(Cameroon).

This NGO is concerned with the collection of data on human rights. It makes public announcements of its activities on radio and television programs.

Reference: US Department of State, *Country Reports of Human Rights Practices for 1993* (Washington, D.C.: Government Printing Office, 1997).

CAMPAIGN FOR DEMOCRACY (CD). (Nigeria).

CD is an umbrella human rights organization that is openly critical of military regimes in Nigeria. General Ibrahim Babangida, who came to power in a 1985 coup, was the head of the military regime until August 1993. General elections were arranged to elect a president on June 12, 1993. Before formal elections were announced, Babangida annulled the June 12 results. Nigerians in the southwest organized civil disobedience campaigns. The government charged the protestors with conspiracy. One member of the CD, Panaf Obkanmi, was detained. Earlier in 1992-93, the CD complained that the security forces had detained and harassed political demonstrators. This group, an amalgamation of diverse volunteer groups cutting across political and ideological lines, worked for democratic and human rights throughout Nigeria. When General Babangida canceled elections in June 1993, the CD's chairman, Beke Ransome-Kuti, protested the subversion of popular will. The CD, to advocate civil rights, called for the release of activists and the reopening of closed media houses. In 1994, the leaders of the CD were arrested and detained for long periods without trial. The activities of the CD were most effective in the urban centers of the south especially in Lagos and among major Yoruba political elites.

References: Julius O. Ihonvbere, "Are Things Falling Apart?," *Journal of Modern African Studies*, 34 (2): 1996: 193-226; John A. Wisemen (ed.), *Democracy and Political Change in Sub-Saharan Africa* (London: Routledge, 1995).

CATHOLIC COMMISSION FOR JUSTICE AND PEACE IN MOZAMBIQUE (COMMISSAO CATOLICA DE JUSTICA E PAZ). (Mozambique).

Small groups of priests and lay people conducted training sessions to prepare the people for the exercise of the democratic vote in 1994. This organization, led by Father Jose Angel, worked also for the eradication of injustices. With limited resources, but actively encouraged by Father Jose Angel, the Catholic Commission concentrated on social and economic rights. It took up cases of nonpayment of salaries as well as unjust dismissals in factories. Now its aim is to extend work to the documentation and denunciation of the arbitrary behavior of the police. However, it lacks staff and resources for the compilation of data.

Reference: University of Minnesota Human Rights Library, "Human Rights" http://www.umn.edu/humanrts/africa.mozambique.htm

CATHOLIC COMMISSION FOR JUSTICE AND PEACE IN ZIMBABWE (CCJPZ). (Zimbabwe).

As a Commission of the Zimbabwe Catholic Bishops Conference, the CCJPZ has been monitoring human rights developments since the beginning of the bush war in the 1970s. It remains politically detached and offers accurate information. This organization had been actively monitoring human rights since independence to establish the whereabouts of the "disappeared." On April 19, 1988, under an amnesty enacted to strengthen the unification of two major parties, the Mugabe government released many political prisoners. The CCJPZ did not receive any complaints of torture in 1988. But between 1983 and 1987, many former Zimbabwe African People's Union (ZAPU) party supporters, who were political dissidents, were imprisoned. According to the CCJPZ, there were about 235 people in this category. Some of them had been put to death by the government. The CCJPZ has criticized the general amnesty for pardoning Government Security agents but arresting suspected dissidents, who were kept in detention for political activities.

Reference: Manfred Nowak and T. Swinehart (eds.), *Human Rights in Developing Countries, 1989 Yearbook* (Strasbourg, Germany: N.P. Engel Publisher, 1989).

CATHOLIC COMMISSION ON JUSTICE AND PEACE (CCJP). (Zambia).

The government of President Chiluba accused this Catholic

church group of having incited people by adapting populist positions on human rights. This Lusaka-based group argues that the major problem of Zambia is poverty. It calls for a wider public debate on alleviating poverty. This organization of Catholic churches has been a victim of police harassment.

Reference: Human Rights Watch, *Zambia* (New York: Human Rights Watch, 1997).

CENTER FOR HUMAN RIGHTS AND HUMANITARIAN LAW (CDH). (Democratic Republic of Congo, formerly Zaire).

The CDH was founded by a group of lawyers in 1992 when this Lubumbashi-based organization assumed the pivotal role in exposing abuses, in pressing for accountability, and in mediating between victims and the government. During the power vacuum in 1995, the National Service of Intelligence and Protection (SNIP), and its head Mate, with the support of Civil Guard, launched a crackdown on dissidents and many youth activists were jailed. The CDH complained against Mate and the government of Zaire and sought to intervene on behalf of detainees. The organization was targeted by the government for having sent letters of complaint to authorities in Kinshasa. On July 31, 1997, the CDH staff visited detainees held at the headquarters of the new political police. In an open letter, the CDH denounced the arbitrary detention of 89 individuals, and the torture and beatings of suspects. Occasionally, the government threatened to arrest the head of the CDH, Jean Mbuyu, and to close down its office. Currently, this group has three full-time investigators.

References: Human Rights Watch, *Zaire* (New York: Human Rights Watch, 1997); Human Rights Watch, http://www.hro

CENTER FOR HUMAN RIGHTS LEGAL AID (CHRLA). (Egypt).

This nongovernmental Cairo-based human rights organization was founded by Hisham Mubarak in 1994. Its contact with Egyptian newspapers, magazines, and Egyptian human rights organizations raised its status. Freedom of expression, including press freedom, faced challenges in 1997 from several quarters. Scholars at al-Azhar Sunni Islamic University fueled a climate of intimidation and physical damage for Egyptian intellectuals. The CHRLA is critical of these intimidation tactics and issues press releases in favor of freedom of expression. It argues that a respected university should not give license to fanatical Islamists to kill people. The group, while acknowledging that the exercise of free expression should not conflict with protection of public morals, pointed out that some penal codes served to intimidate writers. Currently, its work includes presenting reports, issuing press releases, and recording violations of basic freedoms.

References: Human Rights Watch, *World Report 1998* (New York: The Center for Human Rights Legal Aid, 1998); CHRLA home page, http://www.chrla.org/

CENTER FOR LAW RESEARCH INTERNATIONAL (CLARION). (Kenya).

Both Public Order and Societies Acts seriously restricted free human rights organizations and according to law, all organizations were required to register. The CLARION, a legal affairs NGO, was deregistered in 1995 because of its investigations of corruption.

Reference: US Department of State, *Country Reports of Human Rights Practices for 1993* (Washington, D.C.: Government Printing Office, 1994).

CENTER OF OBSERVATION AND PROMOTION OF THE RULE OF LAW. (Togo).

This private group investigates human rights abuses. It complains that the government does not follow up on investigations of abuses in Togo.

Reference: US Department of State, *Country Reports of Human Rights Practices for 1993* (Washington, D.C.: Government Printing Office, 1994).

CENTRAL AFRICAN HUMAN RIGHTS LEAGUE (LCDH). (Central African Republic).

This NGO has several goals, including publicizing human rights violations and pleading individual cases of human rights abuses before the judicial courts. The LCDH distributed its factual pamphlets describing individual rights and judicial procedures to the prisons, police stations, courts, schools, and other NGOs. In May 1996, the LCDH criticized the government's harassment of the press, excessive pretrial detentions in violations of the law, summary executions of suspected bandits, and deaths of suspects while in police custody in Bangui.

Reference: US Department of State, *Country Reports of Human Rights Practices for 1993* (Washington, D.C.: Government Printing Office, 1994).

CHADIAN ASSOCIATION FOR THE PROMOTION AND DEFENSE OF HUMAN RIGHTS. (Chad).

This civic organization took part in commissions investigating human rights abuses in Chad. In the past, it regularly criticized the government for human rights abuses. Now it has some liberty to operate.

Reference: US Department of State, *Country Reports on Human Rights Practices for 1993* (Washington, D.C.: Government Printing Office, 1994).

CHADIAN HUMAN RIGHTS LEAGUE. (Chad).

This organization monitors political torture and detention as well as ill treatment of prisoners. In 1994, two members of the Chadian Human Rights League received death threats from suspected government agents.

Reference: Amnesty International USA, *Amnesty International Report, 1996* (New York: Amnesty International Publications, 1996).

CHILD WELFARE SOCIETY IN KENYA (CWSK). (Kenya).

There are about 40,000 street children who live miserably on main streets in Kenya, and over half of them are in Nairobi city. The government police consider them criminals. The CWSK pleads with the government to address the deep-rooted and complex factors that contribute to their minimal existence on the streets. The society believes that the government must take steps to address the mistreatment of street children by law enforcement authorities. In 1996, the CWSK reported that in Nairobi alone there were thousands of street children and the government treated these children cruelly. This group, in collaboration with external agencies, worked to encourage the establishment of a network for documenting and reporting police violence and abuses against these street children in Kenya, and to follow up with individual cases. In 1995, the group was headed by Kimaru Wakaruru, who actively sought to remedy the situation.

References: Human Rights Watch, *Juvenile Injustice* (New York: Human Rights Watch, 1997); US Department of State, *Country Reports of Human Rights Practices for 1993* (Washington, D.C.: Government Printing Office, 1994).

CHILDREN OF THE VICTIMS OF CAMP BOIRO. (Guinea).

This NGO is concerned with the fate of children of persons who suffered at the hands of the police because of their political beliefs.

Reference: US Department of State, *Country Reports of Human Rights Practices for 1993* (Washington, D.C.: Government Printing Office, 1994).

CHRISTIAN COUNCIL OF MOZAMBIQUE (CONSELHO CRISTAO DE MOCAMBIQUE) (CCM). (Mozambique).

This NGO is concerned with varied social and religious issues in Mozambique. The CCM, organized by Protestants as well as syncretic Christians, is less concerned with strictly legal issues and "first generation" rights, and more concerned with economic empowerment of the poor. Communities are asked to speak out on issues such as low wages, unemployment, the abuse of authority, and the lack of access to land. The CCM gets advice from the **Mozambique League of Human Rights**.

Reference: University of Minnesota Human Rights Library, "Human Rights," http://www.umn.edu/humanrts/africa.mozambique.htm

CIVIL LIBERTIES ORGANIZATION (CLO). (Nigeria).

There was hardly any human rights group in Nigeria until October 1987, when the CLO was founded by some lawyers, led by Olisa Agbakoba. Before 1987, Nigerians were more concerned with ethnic and regional organizations than any national movement for human rights. When General Ibrahim Babangida annulled general election results, there was political unrest and the Nigerian federal government arrested many protesters. The CLO acted as a political opposition group and at the same time upheld the issues related to civil and political rights of citizens. In recent reports it has claimed that scores of people died annually while in police custody. The reports, went on to allege that the police used torture to extract confessions. The CLO publicized the case of Johnny

Eshict, who died in police custody in September 1992. Also it was reported by the CLO that police had arrested and beaten two people after they filed a complaint with the police. In another case, the police in Port Harcourt chained the hands and feet of detained Madufurio Igwe and suspended him upside down from a ceiling fan. The CLO reported these human rights abuses.

Reference: Julius O. Ihonvbere, "Are Things Falling Apart?," *Journal of Modern African Studies*, 34 (2), 1996: 193-226.

COALITION AGAINST SLAVERY IN MAURITANIA AND SUDAN (CASMAS). (USA).

This American-based private human rights organization has many members from Africans in Africa and African-Americans in the United States. Dedicated to fighting African enslavement, it has been concerned with the present tragedy of chattel slavery in Mauritania and Sudan. Even now, black Africans are bought and sold in these two countries. Black slaves are given as wedding gifts, traded for camels, guns, trucks, and even inherited. This organization gives publicity to these tragic cases of modern slavery by writing articles and through other means of publicity.

Reference: CASMAS Home Page, 1998: http://www.cc.columbia.edu/slc11/

COLLECTIF. (Niger).

Representing varied political views, this umbrella association was created to promote human rights as well as democracy in Niger. It has been critical of the government's defective organization and management of presidential elections.

Reference: US Department of State, *Country Reports of Human Rights Practices for 1993* (Washington, D.C.: Government Printing Office, 1994).

COLLECTIVE OF FAMILIES SEPARATED BY DEPORTATION (CFSD). (Mauritania).

The CFSD was organized by a group of some 22 lawyers representing families of victims of ethnic purges by the Mauritanian military. President Maaouya Ould Sid'Ahmed Taya began his rule of Mauritania in 1984, first as head of the military junta, and then as head of an elected civilian government. The 1989 crisis led to approximately 13,000 Mauritanian Peuhl (Fulani) to take refuge in Mali. Of the 60,000 African-Mauritanians who were expelled, about 56,000 remained in refugee camp in Senegal. The CFSD represented the spouses (mainly women) and children of persons who were deported to Senegal during the 1989 crisis. More than 500 black Mauritanians were executed without trial or due process during 1990. Members of the Collective have tried to seek redress for those affected by the purges and mass killings. The government, meanwhile, has taken various steps to impede the judicial process and block the Collective's efforts.

References: US Department of State, *Country Reports of Human Rights Practices for 1993* (Washington, D.C.: Government Printing Office, 1994*)*; Lawyers Committee for Human Rights, *In Defense of Rights: Attacks on Lawyers and Judges in 1993* (New York: Lawyers Committee for Human Rights, 1993).

COLLECTIVE OF SURVIVORS OF POLITICAL DETENTION AND TORTURE (CRAPOCIT). (Mauritania).

This collective was established in 1996 to seek redress for abuses committed during the 1986-87 period. Currently, it operates openly and actively, but is not officially recognized. The CRAPOCIT focuses on the sufferings of the victims of the 1990-91 military purge and their families.

Reference: US Department of State, *Country Reports of Human Rights Practices for 1993* (Washington, D.C.: Government Printing Office, 1994).

COLLECTIVE OF WORKERS VICTIMS. (Mauritania).

Although not officially recognized, this private group seeks remedies for the families that suffered in 1989 during political disturbances. This small group called for financial compensation for the loss of jobs by workers. It considered the right to work a human rights issue.

Reference: US Department of State, *Country Reports of Human Rights Practices for 1993* (Washington, D.C.: Government Printing Office, 1994).

COMMISSION FOR THE POPULARIZATION OF FUNDAMENTAL RIGHTS OF THE EVANGELICAL

LUTHERAN CHURCH IN ZAIRE. (Democratic Republic of Congo, formerly Zaire).

This church-based NGO is an example of links between the regional churches and human rights organizations. It is engaged in activities such as confrontation of such problems as public insecurity or generalized practice by corrupt state agents of over-inflating public utility bills. The Commission took part in the nation-wide protests in 1992 for democracy and freedom of political activity.

Reference: Human Rights Watch, *Zaire* (New York, Human Rights Watch: 1997).

COMMISSION ON HUMAN RIGHTS AND ADMINISTRATIVE JUSTICE (CHRAJ). (Ghana).

Generally, government-financed national commissions have been ineffective in reporting human rights abuses in Africa. The activities of Ghana's CHRAJ received wide publicity and showed how such government-controlled bodies, even when initially created by a government, can develop lives of their own. It was designed in 1993 to deal with human rights issues and violations of individual rights. Gradually, this body became autonomous and was empowered to investigate human rights violations and to take appropriate action to remedy proven abuses.

References: LaVerle Berry (ed.), *Ghana: A Country Study* (Washington, D.C.: Government Printing Office, 1995); New York: Human Rights Watch, *World Report 1998* (New York: Human Rights Watch, 1998).

COMMITTEE AGAINST TORTURE. (Algeria).

After 1987, the Algerian government gave approval to a few NGOs to report on rights violations. After getting legal status, this small group investigated allegations of torture. It was able to publicize its findings and publish reports on the treatment of political detainees. Currently, this group monitors cases of torture and extra-judicial killings committed by both government and opposition Armed Islamist Groups. The Armed Islamist Groups committed grave human rights abuses during 1993 in Algeria, killing over 150 civilians. The Committee reported these cases.

References: Helen C. Metz (ed.), *Algeria: A Country Study* (Washington, D.C.: Government Printing Office, 1994); Amnesty

International USA, *Amnesty International Report, 1994* (New York: Amnesty International Publications, 1994).

COMMITTEE FOR A CLEAN CAMPAIGN (CCC). (Zambia).
This civic group was set up to work for free and fair elections in Zambia. The Chiluba government accused the Campaign of obtaining funds from foreign governments between 1991 and 1996, and so the government raided its Lusaka offices. The police froze the bank accounts of the organization.

Reference: Human Rights Watch, *Zambia* (New York: Human Rights Watch: 1997).

COMMITTEE FOR THE DEFENCE OF HUMAN RIGHTS (CDHR). (Nigeria).
This private society deals with custodial/post-trial rights in Nigeria. It tries to prevent torture or any other inhumane or degrading treatment. In 1990, the then Lagos State Governor, Raji Rasaki, announced immediate execution of some minor boys, who were accused of committing a serious crime. A judge dismissed the government's objections that the judge had no jurisdiction to hear a suit by the twelve juveniles. Because of protests from the CDHR, **Civil Liberties Organization,** and other NGOs, the boys' death sentences were commuted to life imprisonment. In 1991, the CDHR issued reports on why General Obasanjo was ineligible for the post of UN Secretary General. When General Ibrahim Babangida canceled presidential election results, the CDHR urged Nigerians to work for democracy as well as for the maintenance of civil rights.

References: M. Cheri Bassiouni and Ziyad Motala (eds.), *The Protection of Human Rights in African Criminal Proceedings* (London: Martinus Publishers, 1995); Civil Liberties Organization, *Ajibola Years* (Lagos: CLO, 1991); Julius O. Ihonvbere, "Are Things Falling Apart?," *Journal of Modern African Studies*, 34 (2), 1996: 193-226.

COMMITTEE FOR THE DEFENSE OF CIVIC RIGHTS (CDCR). (Guinea).
Guinea held its first multiparty elections in 1994 and President Lansana was officially elected. But human rights remained circumscribed despite presidential elections involving eight candidates. The CDCR has been vocal in criticizing the

government for its failure to honor general human rights and as such the government did not welcome the NGOs commentary or investigations of abuses of political opponents.

Reference: US Department of State, *Country Reports of Human Rights Practices for 1993* (Washington, D.C.: Government Printing Office, 1994).

COMMITTEE FOR THE LEGAL EQUALITY OF MEN AND WOMEN. (Algeria).

The government has become increasingly receptive to the role of women in the public realm. Women have joined this small group to better their standing, but the fear of government retaliation kept many women away from this group.

Reference: Helen C. Metz (ed.), *Algeria: A Country Report* (Washington, D.C.: Government Printing Office, 1994).

COMMITTEE FOR UNITY AND PROGRESS IN NIGERIA (CUPN). (Nigeria).

This committee advocates political and civil rights against state tyranny. In addition to suppressing political protests against Structural Adjustment Programs, the Babangida government prevented individuals and organizations from holding conferences designed to articulate means for reforms. In 1989, the CUPN organized a conference. Police raided the convention, and later the police arrested Gani Fawehinmi and other human rights activists.

Reference: Eileen McCarthy-Arnolds et al., *Africa, Human Rights, and the Global System* (Westport, CT: Greenwood Press, 1994).

COMMITTEE OF RELATIVES AND WIVES OF PRISONERS OF CONSCIENCE. (Benin).

This committee was formed in 1986 to campaign for the release of political prisoners in Benin. Its chairman, Jonas Gninmaguou, an activist, was detained in 1986 and the group called for his release on the grounds that he was not politically motivated.

Reference: Amnesty International, *1993 Report* (New York: Amnesty International Publications, 1993).

COMMITTEE OF SOLIDARITY WITH THE VICTIMS OF REPRESSION IN MAURITANIA. (Mauritania).

This committee is concerned with the plight of the 1989 expellees. Its members attended a March 1993 meeting in Banjul of the **International Commission of Jurists**, where they openly aired their grievances about the human rights situation in Mauritania.

Reference: US Department of State, *Country Reports of Human Rights Practices for 1993* (Washington, D.C.: Government Printing Office, 1994).

COMMITTEE OF THE WIDOWS. (Mauritania)
This committee is concerned with the sufferings of the victims of the 1990-91 military purge. It seeks redress for the widows killed during the political disturbances.

Reference: US Department of State, *Country Reports of Human Rights Practices for 1993* (Washington, D.C.: Government Printing Office, 1994).

COMMITTEE ON HUMAN AND PEOPLE'S RIGHTS (CHPR). (Ghana).
Retired Lt. Jerry John Railings seized power in 1981 and then became the first President of the Fourth Republic. Ghanaians exercised their right to vote in 1992. The opposition parties claimed that the presidential election had been fraudulent and that there were no opposition party members in the national parliament. As human rights organizations grew more numerous and vocal in 1993, the CHPR set up branches to monitor human rights issues.

Reference: US Department of State, *Country Reports of Human Rights Practices for 1993* (Washington, D.C.: Government Printing Office, 1994).

COMMITTEE ON TRADITIONAL PRACTICES AFFECTING WOMEN AND CHILDREN (CPTAFE). (Guinea).
This NGO is dedicated to eradicating female genital circumcision in Guinea. It educates health workers.

Reference: US Department of State, *Country Reports of Human Rights Practices for 1993* (Washington, D.C.: Government Printing Office, 1994).

COMMUNITY LAW CENTRE OF THE UNIVERSITY OF THE WESTERN CAPE. (South Africa).

This group works for childrens' and prisoners' rights. A study of children in the criminal justice system in South Africa, *Justice for the Children: No Child Should Be Caged*, was published by the Children's Rights Research and Advocacy Project of the Community Law Centre at the University of the Western Cape, in October 1992.

Reference: Africa Watch, *Prison Conditions in South Africa* (New York: Human Rights Watch, 1994).

COMOROS HUMAN RIGHTS ASSOCIATION (CHRA).
(Comoros).

The Federal Republic of the Comoros has three islands. Until the assassination of President Abdallah in November 1989, the Comoros was in fact a one party state. The Constitution of 1992 provides for the equality of all citizens. Muslim religious leaders tend to dominate local politics. In May 1990, a group of private citizens established the CHRA, which is also known as the **Comorian Association for the Rights of Man**. It reports on unhealthy prison conditions. The CHRA has access to civilian prisons, and in one case has been able to transfer a prisoner, who was mistreated, from the government prison to a mission facility.

Reference: Human Rights Watch, http://www.hrw.org

CONCENTRATION. (Democratic Republic of Congo, formerly Zaire). Concentration is the umbrella forum of all human rights groups in Lubumbashi that act together to raise human rights cases with government and military officials. Its main organizer is Masudi Kingombe, who is being assisted by half a dozen volunteers. Now the organization investigates cases of political detainees.

Reference: Human Rights Watch, http://www.hrw.org

CONCERN. (Rwanda).

This small NGO is engaged in reporting killings by soldiers and police. The Rwandan government does not approve of its actions. In January 1998 soldiers shot at two employees of Concern.

Reference: Human Rights Watch, *World Report 1998* (New York: Human Rights Watch, 1998).

CONCERNED PARENTS ASSOCIATION. (Uganda).

This group of Ugandan parents came together to demand action when their daughters, 139 girls from the St. Mary's School, were abducted by the Lord's Resistance Army in October 1996. The Concerned Parents have worked tirelessly to secure the release of their daughters, and all children in rebel captivity. The group has succeeded in bringing national and international attention to the cause of the victims, and has raised concerns with President Yoweri Museveni. It has been a powerful voice for all children in rebel captivity. Currently, Angelina Acheng Atyam, a nurse-midwife and mother of six, is the vice chair of this NGO.

Reference: Human Rights Watch, *World Report 1998* (New York: Human Rights Watch, 1998).

CONGOLESE ASSOCIATION OF WOMEN LAWYERS. (Republic of Congo).

Although the new Constitution prohibits discrimination based on gender, various hidden discriminations against women are endemic. Marriage and family laws overtly discriminate against women. For example, adultery is illegal for women, but not for men. Violence against women occurs frequently. The Congolese Association of Women Lawyers has criticized the past governmental abuses of human rights and has called for the abolition of discrimination based on traditional customs.

Reference: US Department of State, *Country Reports of Human Rights Practices for 1993* (Washington, D.C : Government Printing Office, 1994).

CONGOLESE HUMAN RIGHTS LEAGUE (CHRL). (Congo).

During 1993 the Republic of Congo's young democracy was severely tried by several episodes of violent civil disturbances. The year saw perpetration of widespread abuses. Militia, loyal to faction leaders, held rival groups hostage and there were many reports of rape, assault, and physical torture. Some members of the President's irregular militia also committed offenses and abuses on political activists. The government ignored calls for investigations regarding extrajudicial killings in 1993. Currently, the League represents the rights of prisoners, women, children, and the handicapped. It freely criticizes the governmental abuses and reports that there are discriminations arising out of traditional local customs.

Reference: US Department of State, *Country Reports of Human Rights Practices for 1993* (Washington, D.C.: Government Printing Office, 1994).

CONSTITUTIONAL RIGHTS PROJECT (CRP). (Nigeria).

To challenge the human rights violations under General Babangida, this group began to work to uphold civil rights. It noted the absence of institutional mechanisms for drawing attention to human rights in Nigeria and conducted a nationwide police powers study that indicated in 1993 that the majority of police rationalized the use of torture of suspects in police custody. It claimed that 67 percent of the officers interviewed conceded that, in the absence of an efficient means of investigating a crime, torture became the easiest means of extracting information from suspects.

Reference: Eileen McCarthy-Arnolds et al., *Africa, Human Rights, and the Global System* (Westport, CT: Greenwood Press, 1994).

CO-ORDINATED ACTION FOR BATTERED WOMEN. (South Africa).

This Johannesburg-based private organization collects accurate data on domestic violence to establish the extent of the problem of battered women. It estimates that one in six women is abused by her partner.

Reference: The Human Rights Watch, *Global Report on Women's Human Rights* (New York: Human Rights Watch, 1995).

D

DEFENDERS OF HUMAN RIGHTS IN TANZANIA. (Tanzania).
This organization was formed to address the concerns of families, the disabled, women, and children — all of whom suffered variously because of the action of the state, particularly the police. The Defenders complain that the Tanzanian government has delayed the registration of their organization. Thus they argue that their access to abused people and the ability to monitor human rights violations have been hampered.
Reference: US Department of State, *Country Reports of Human Rights Practices for 1993* (Washington, D.C.: Government Printing Office, 1997).

DEMOCRACY, LIBERTY, AND DEVELOPMENT (DLD). (Niger).
The DLD operates without explicit governmental hindrances, although an atmosphere of intimidation has prevailed. It investigates cases of civil rights violations as well as gross violations of human rights. It upholds the cause of democracy as well.
Reference: US Department of State, *Country Reports of Human Rights Practices for 1993* (Washington, D.C.: Government Printing Office, 1994).

DETAINEES' PARENTS SUPPORT COMMITTEE (DPSC). (South Africa).

This was a church organization in the so-called "independent" homeland of Venda in northern Transvaal. Popular opposition to the harsh and corrupt rule of the black homeland leaders was apparent in the 1980s and many church leaders opposing the Venda government were physically threatened. According to a memo from the DPSC, two Lutheran Ministers were badly treated by the Venda National Force. One Minister was forced to do arduous physical exercises and was taunted and mocked. One Reverend was "deported" from Venda. This group is concerned with these rights abuses. In 1982, it published a "Memorandum on Security Police Abuses of Political Detainees" in which the group alleged that systematic and wide spread torture in detention centers — hooding, partial suffocation, infliction of electric shock, and beatings with fists — was not reported. Arguing that the ill treatment of ordinary suspects was a breach of human rights in South Africa, the DPSC called for adequate safeguards to protect detainees and for an enforceable code of interrogation practices.

References: Human Rights Watch / An Africa Watch Report, *No Neutral Ground: South Africa's Confrontation with the Activist Churches* (New York: Human Rights Watch, 1989); Amnesty International, *Torture in the Eighties* (London: Amnesty International, 1984).

DEVELOPMENT ALTERNATIVES WITH WOMEN FOR A NEW ERA (DAWN). (Italy).

Despite the evidence that African women produce approximately 60% of the food consumed by rural Africa, neither national nor international agricultural resources are directed toward women in the continent. As a result, an international women's group was set up to work in collaboration with the Food and Agricultural Organization in Rome. This women's group in many developing countries took an empowerment approach in the mid-1980s. Its African founding members were Fatima Mernissi of Morocco, Achola Pala Okeyo of Kenya, and Marie-Angelique of Senegal. The group is engaged in women's access to productive resources such as land, credit, and training.

References: Gita Sen and Caren Crown, *Development, Crises and Alternative Visions* (New York: Monthly Review Press, 1987); *Africa Today* (Denver, CO.:1990), p. 36-37.

DEVELOPMENT WORKSHOP. (Angola).

The Angolan government did not encourage local human rights monitoring, and as such this independent Angolan NGO distributed information about human rights without much publicity. This group worked with fishermen and market women in Luanda to improve their knowledge of basic political rights.

Reference: Human Rights Watch, *World Report 1998* (New York: Human Rights Watch, 1998).

DISABLED PEOPLE SOUTH AFRICA (DPSA). (South Africa).

During the election in 1994, this group argued that polling stations should architecturally be accessible to wheelchair using voters. Its main goal is to fight for all including disabled persons.

Reference: US Department of State, *Country Reports on Human Rights Practices for 1993* (Washington, D.C.: Government Printing Office, 1994).

DJIBOUTIAN NATIONAL WOMEN'S UNION (DNWU).
(Djibouti).

Since independence in 1977, the country remained a de facto one-party state. In 1993, President Hassan Gouled Aptidon and his party, the People's Rally, controlled aspects of civil and political life. Although the government welcomed some international organizations to look into human rights, it was disdainful of domestic human rights groups. In 1988, the DNWU began an educational campaign against the practice of female genital mutilation, particularly infibulation, the most dangerous and extensive form of mutilation in Djibouti, which is generally performed on girls between the age of 7 and 10. The government has passed a law against the mutilation, but no one has been convicted under the law. The DNWU is concerned with these abuses.

Reference: US Department of State, *Country Reports of Human Rights Practices for 1993* (Washington, D.C.: Government Printing Office, 1994).

E

EGYPTIAN BAR ASSOCIATION. (Egypt).

This private group defends clients accused of membership in illegal Islamist opposition groups. It is based in Asyut, a city in southern Egypt that has been a center of political violence between armed Islamist Groups and the Egyptian Security forces. Al-Touni, chairman of the Civil Liberties' Committee of the Asyut branch of the Egyptian Bar Association, was detained in 1992 and tried by military courts. The Egyptian Bar Association argued that military courts had illegally superseded the jurisdiction of the civilian judiciary, and as such military courts violated human rights of the defendants.

Reference: Lawyers Committee for Human Rights, *In Defense of Human Rights* (New York: Lawyers Committee for Human Rights, 1993).

EGYPTIAN ORGANIZATION FOR HUMAN RIGHTS (EOHR). (Egypt).

The EOHR was founded in 1985 as a premier NGO working for the support and defense of human rights in Egypt. It applied for registration in July 1987 in accordance with the requirement of the Egyptian Law 32 of 1964, but to date it has failed to obtain the government's permission to operate without interference. Because it does not "legally" exist, the EOHR cannot hold public meetings in its own name. Currently, it works out of the Cairo headquarters of its parent organization, the **Arab Organization for Human Rights**

(AOHR). The EOHR claimed that since the late 1980s, there was a marked increase of torture not only against members of subversive organizations but also against ordinary citizens with no political affiliations. In April 1991, it applied again to the court for legal status but the Egyptian court rejected its petition. However, the organization has developed an extensive network of international relations. Its reports are cited by international organizations working on Egypt, and by the United States Department of State in the section on Egypt in its annual *Country Reports on Human Rights Practices*. Through its link to the AOHR, this Egyptian organization has obtained consultative status with the UN Economic and Social Council and the African Commission on Human and Peoples' Rights. It is also the only Middle East based member of the International Freedom of Expression Exchange, which is run by the Canadian Committee to Protect Journalists. Currently, it urges Egyptian authorities to revise all laws that are not in line with international human rights standards, and it calls on the government to stop all practices that disregard human rights as prescribed by the International Covenant on Civil and Political Rights. In March 1997, the EOHR expressed concern about reports that in Upper Egypt the security forces had armed civilians to guard government buildings and to search and detain suspects. The group warned that a cycle of violence could be set in motion if the government used armed civilians as substitutes for police. In recent months, this group has documented wholly inadequate medical care of prison inmates.

References: Louis Henkin and John Lawrence Hargrove (eds.), *Human Rights: An Agenda for the Next Century* (Washington, D.C.: The American Society of International Law, 1994); EOHR, *Lawyers Committee for Human Rights: North Africa* (Giza, Egypt: Lawyers Committee for Human Rights, 1991); http://www.eorg.org.eg/Docs/what.htm (EOHR home page).

EMANG BASADI (Stand Up Women). (Botswana).
In the early 1990s, this group of professional women disputed the Botswana Citizenship Law that legitimized the dominant rule of men in society. In 1990, one of its members, Unity Dow, a lawyer, took the government to court over the citizenship law, which, she claimed, limited women's basic

rights and freedoms. The Emang Basadi group demanded equal participation and representation by women via the development of strategies that would change the existing social structures.

Reference: Gisela Geisler, "Troubled Sisterhood," *African Affairs, no. 94* (1995), pp. 36-37.

ERITREAN RELIEF ASSOCIATION (ERA). (Eritrea).

This society provided relief to war victims as well as victims of natural calamities. At the same time, it called for the observance of human rights in Eritrea. It was the only humanitarian organization working in areas of Eritrea not held by the Ethiopian central government. In 1978, the ERA transported resources from northeast Sudan into areas controlled by its parent armies. This semi-autonomous relief agency asked for the maintenance of general rights in war torn areas of Ethiopia.

Reference: Eileen McCarthy-Arnolds et al., *Africa, Human Rights, and the Global System* (Westport, CT: Greenwood Press, 1994).

ETHIOPIAN HUMAN RIGHTS COUNCIL (EHRCO). (Ethiopia).

Since the overthrow of Mengistu Haile Mariam, a few human rights organizations began to emerge in Ethiopia. In contrast to the Mengistu years, the human rights situation in Ethiopia has improved. But the new government has shown increasing intolerance of political dissidents; it has invoked the Criminal Code to harass opponents. Several officials of the EHRCO were arrested. Up to 1993, the EHRCO did not get any permit from the government for legal operation. With highly limited economic resources and with widespread popular expectations for major improvements in civil liberties in Ethiopia, this organization led by Mesfin Wolde Mariam, a retired professor of geography, began to highlight abuses. The EHRCO's declared aims were promotion of democracy, maintenance of basic human rights, and the rule of law. In fact, Mesfin Wolde Mariam regarded human right activism as an extension of his research. In 1984, he published *Rural Vulnerability to Famine in Ethiopia 1958-77*, a technical study with important human rights overtones. Antagonism between the Ethiopian government and the EHRCO soon came to the surface. Each EHRCO report included details of complaints sent to it by

EHRCO staff. Some argued that the EHRCO's allegations were incomplete or inaccurate, largely as a result of the secrecy that shrouded wide areas of Ethiopian life. But the human rights council submitted that its reports were not without substance. In the recent past, the group has provided both a voice for the rule of law as well as an outlet for reporting the abuses of the Transitional Government of Ethiopia and the opposition. Reports of the EHRCO could not be easily brushed aside, although there were occasional errors. Its fifth report cited instances of extra-judicial killings, torture, disappearances, unlawful police detentions, and other violations by the Ethiopian government. There are now intense rivalries among human rights groups — Forum-84, the Centre for Human Rights and Democracy, etc. On December 1, 1997, the EHRCO reported that the extra-judicial killings of Ato Tereffe Qumbi, Ato Tesfaye Kumisa, and Captain Gudisa Insa (all prisoners of conscience) took place in violation of universal human rights.

References: Claude E. Welch, *Protecting Human Rights in Africa* (Philadelphia: University of Pennsylvania Press, 1995); *Ethiopian Herald* (July 18, 1993); Mesfin Wolde-Mariam, *Suffering Under God's Environment: A Vertical Study of Peasants in North-Central Ethiopia* (Berne: African Mountain Association, Geographica Bernesia, 1991); Swedish NGO Foundation for Human Rights, *The Status of Human Rights Organizations in Sub-Saharan Africa* (Stockholm: The International Human Rights Internship Program Publications, 1994).

ETHIOPIAN RIGHTS COUNCIL. (Ethiopia).
This self-proclaimed human rights monitoring organization operates with legal status as an NGO. The government considers it primarily as a political organization.

Reference: US Department of State, *Country Reports on Human Rights Practices for 1996* (Washington, D.C.: Government Printing Office, 1997).

ETHIOPIAN WOMEN LAWYERS ASSOCIATION. (Ethiopia).
While women's status and political participation are greater than ever, there are areas where more work needs to be done. This group of lawyers tries to improve social status of Ethiopian women.

Reference: US Department of State, *Country Reports on Human Rights*

Practices for 1996 (Washington, D.C.: Government Printing Office, 1997).

ETHNIC MINORITY RIGHTS ORGANIZATION OF AFRICA (EMRROAF). (Nigeria).

To promote democracy and uphold human rights, this local private organization in the 1990s sought to cut across communal and class lines in Nigeria. It served a critical role in public education on human rights. Ken Saro-Wiwa, who was president of the **MOSOP**, was also president of the EMRROAF. He was a committed defender of minority rights, and used his connections with the media and international human rights and environmental protection organizations to pursue the Ogoni people's case in Nigeria.

References: John A. Wiseman (ed.), *Democracy and Political Change in Sub-Saharan Africa* (London: Routledge, 1995); Eghosa A. Osaghae, "The Ogoni Uprising," *African Affairs*, 94: (1995); pp. 27-34.

F

FEDERATION OF GHANAIAN WOMEN LAWYERS ASSOCIATION (FIDA). (Ghana).

The FIDA is an emerging human rights group, run by women. It devotes Wednesdays to providing free legal advice to women who need it on human rights issues. With the support of the Geneva-based International Commission of Jurists, the FIDA established a legal aid advice service in Accra, Ghana in 1984. Its emphasis is on the empowerment of women and as such it operates with the assumption that women should be given education and legal aid so that "more women are able to seek prompt assistance if any of their rights are violated."

Reference: International Commission of Jurists, *Paralegals in Rural Africa* (Geneva, Switzerland: International Commission of Jurists, 1991).

FEDERATION OF WOMEN'S LAWYERS IN GAMBIA. (Gambia).

This NGOs main preoccupation has been to find a reasonable means to transmit knowledge of rights and duties to the wider population in the Gambia. In its training center, teachers are expected to design the curriculum and the training materials by beginning from what the people already know. The organization has tried to empower people in rural areas to become aware of human rights as the fundamental principles of human social relations.

Reference: Brendalyn P. Ambrose, *Democratization and the Promotion* *of Human Rights in Africa: Problems and Prospects* (Westport, CT: Praeger, 1995).

FEDERATION OF WOMEN'S LAWYERS IN NIGERIA. (Nigeria).
The organization has made progress toward training paralegals, who are expected to train people in human rights. It offers nonformal educational programs.
Reference: International Commission of Jurists, *Paralegals in Rural Africa* (Geneva: International Commission of Jurists, 1991).

FORO MULHER. (Mozambique).
This is an umbrella organization for women's NGOs. It has 21 registered members and highlights a variety of women's issues, including domestic violence, legal inequities, and economic empowerment. It also provides basic legal advice for abused women. Its effectiveness is not apparent because it mostly operates in towns like Maputo, but the majority of violent abuses against women takes place in rural areas.
Reference: US Department of State, *Country Reports on Human Rights for 1996* (Washington, D.C.: Government Printing Office, 1997).

FORUM FOR THE RESTORATION OF DEMOCRACY (FORD). (Kenya).
The Forum first met on March 19, 1992, under the leadership of a group of women who were on a hunger strike. They camped in Uhuru Park in Nairobi, staging their protest against the detention of their husbands, sons, and friends. In 1993, its vice-chairman was beaten by police because of his demonstration to protest the economic situation in Kenya. One of the strategies of this group is to hold seminars on the resettlement of victims of politically instigated ethnic clashes in Kenya.
References: *African Woman* (July-October 1992); Lawyers Committee for Human Rights, *In Defense of Rights: Attacks on Lawyers and Judges in 1993* (New York: Lawyers Committee for Human Rights, 1993).

FOUNDATION FOR DEMOCRACY IN ZIMBABWE (FODEZI). (Zimbabwe).
The Foundation was established in July 1996 as a watchdog organization to support independent candidates in elections. To promote multiparty democracy, this civic and human rights

group works to monitor rights violations during general elections.

Reference: US Department of State, *Country Reports on Human Rights for 1993* (Washington, D.C.: Government Printing Office, 1997).

FOUNDATION OF DEMOCRATIC PROCESS (FODEP). (Zambia).

The new 1991 Constitution prohibited torture as a means of investigation, but members of the police and security service regularly used excessive force when apprehending, interrogating, and holding criminal suspects or illegal aliens. In 1993, the government permitted delegations of the FODEP to visit 10 of the detainees at two separate prisons. The group, along with YWCA, became active in promoting women's social and political rights.

Reference: US Department of State, *Country Reports on Human Rights Practices for 1993* (Washington, D.C.: Government Printing Office, 1994).

FOUNDATION OF HUMAN RIGHTS INITIATIVE (FHRI). (Uganda).

Of ten important NGOs, four actively monitor human rights cases in Uganda. In October 1993, the FHRI published the first edition of its journal, *The Human Rights Defenders.*

Reference: US Department of State, *Country Reports on Human Rights Practices for 1993* (Washington, D.C.: Government Printing Office, 1994).

FREE LEGAL ASSISTANCE GROUP (FLAG). (Democratic Republic of Congo, formerly Zaire).

This group provides information regarding human rights violation to the African Commission. Concerned with complaints of massive violations, the African Commission asked for permission to visit Zaire. But no response came from the government.

Reference: U. O. Umozurike, *Self-Determination in International Law* (Hamden, CT: Archon, 1972); U. O. Umozurike, "The Protection of Human Rights Under the Banjul African Charter on Human and Peoples' Rights," *African Journal of International Law* 1 (1988), 65-83

FRIENDS OF NELSON MANDELA. (Democratic Republic of

Congo, formerly Zaire).

Concerned with disappearances of people in civil war torn
Zaire, this Kishangani based nongovernmental monitoring
group reported the disappearance of Damadu Mbula, who was
never located. The group complained that these
disappearances were the result of the political beliefs of the
dissidents.

Reference: US Department of State, *Country Reports on Human Rights
Practices for 1993* (Washington, D.C.: Government Printing Office,
1994).

G

GABONESE LEAGUE OF HUMAN RIGHTS (GLHR). (Gabon). President Bongo's term will expire in 1999. While his government handles most human rights cases, it also permits private groups to report on human rights violations. One such group is the GLHR, which claimed in 1993 that its leader was harassed after a broadcast on Radio Liberte in which he had attacked the Communications Minister for suspending the independent press.

Reference: US Department of State, *Country Reports on Human Rights Practices for 1993* (Washington, D.C.: Government Printing Office, February 1994).

GANI FAWEHINMI SOLIDARITY ASSOCIATION IN NIGERIA (GFSA). (Nigeria).

This solidarity group, which has been operating since 1987, has been working under the umbrella organization called the **Campaign for Democracy (CD)**, which has been persistent in calling for the restoration of civil and political rights, and open society in Nigeria. Chief Gani Fawehinmi completed legal studies in London, returned to Nigeria, and built a lucrative legal practice. He prided himself on being the leading legal gadfly of the Ibrahim Babangida government, filing suits to challenge the "ouster clauses" whereby the constitution was suspended and courts were enjoined from enforcing basic rights. Gani Fawehinmi, an advocate of human rights and a social crusader, was disturbed that virtually all of the assaults on human rights that made apartheid in South Africa a pariah in the world were also broadly practiced in Nigeria under military rule. Gani's troubles with the government began in 1987 when he went to court to prosecute Col. Halilu Akilu, director of military intelligence. He asked for respect for fundamental human rights, the rule of law, and abrogation of rule by government decree. Gani was arrested in May 1992 and charged with treasonable felony after Gani, along with others, called for a national conference to address the varied problems confronting Nigeria's basic rights issues. Although the court ordered Gani's release, the government kept the protesters in jail for almost a month. The society named after him continued to report abuses committed during the administration of General Ibrahim Babangida.

References: Claude E. Welch, *Protecting Human Rights in Africa* (Philadelphia: University of Pennsylvania Press, 1995); Eileen McCarthy-Arnolds et al., *Africa, Human Rights, and the Global System* (Westport, CT: Greenwood Press, 1994); Brendalyn P. Ambrose, *Democratization and the Protection of Human Rights in Africa* (Westport, CT: Praeger, 1995); *A Harvest of Violations: Annual Report on Human Rights in Nigeria, 1991* (Lagos: Civil Liberties Organization; 1992); C. Gahia, *Human Rights in Retreat* (Lagos: Civil Liberties Organization, 1993).

GHANA ASSOCIATION FOR THE WELFARE OF WOMEN (GAWW). (Ghana).

This emerging human rights association is administered by women in Ghana. The basic philosophy of this association is that women have experienced oppression in their roles as workers by classism, as blacks by racism, and as women by patriarchy. It commissioned a report on female genital operations prevalent in the country and has since been actively working to end the practice.

References: George W. Shepherd, Jr., and Mark O. Anikpo (eds.), *Emerging Human Rights* (Westport, CT.: Greenwood Press, 1990); John Kardi, *The Practice of Female Circumcision in the Upper East Region of Ghana* (Accra, Ghana: Ghanaian Association for Women's Welfare, 1986).

GHANA BAR ASSOCIATION. (GBA). (Ghana).

Following the military coup in December 1981 by Lt. Jerry Rawlings, this bar association began to uphold people' civil and political rights. It sharply reacted to the PNDC's (the military ruling council) attempt to curtail basic freedoms and regarded these interferences as infringements on human rights. During the early 1980s, it concentrated on the due release of political prisoners. Specifically, it called for the early release of detainees held under the Preventive Custody Law. It asked for the repeal of this law. It criticized the government's use of public tribunals in the administration of justice. In 1989, the government detained the president and secretary of the bar association because they refused to accept government funding for an African Bar Association Conference in Accra. The government cancelled the conference. Its objectives have been: the maintenance of judicial independence to protect human rights and fundamental freedoms, as defined under the **United Nations Declarations on Human Rights**. The GBA has a specific committee called Ghana Bar Association Human Rights Committee.

References: LaVerle Berry (ed.), *Ghana: A Country Study* (Washington, D.C., Government Printing Office, 1995); Jeff Haynes, "Human Rights and Democracy in Ghana," *African Affairs* (1991).

GHANA COMMITTEE ON HUMAN AND PEOPLE'S RIGHTS (GCHPR). (Ghana).

Founded in early January 1991, this group of dedicated lawyers, trade unionists, and journalists, has perhaps been the most successful human rights organization in Ghana. It desires to watch for and to publicize violations of basic human freedoms, namely the right to free press, free movement, and unhindered right to assembly and organization. It has been credited with contributing to an improved human rights climate in the early 1990s. In 1993, the group presented an eleven-page report to the **African Commission**, giving some background information on the human rights record of Ghanaian dictatorial regimes that had ruled the country since independence. The report noted that although Ghana ratified the African Charter, no steps had been taken to make the African Charter part of the municipal law. The report concluded that although some steps had already been taken by the Fourth Republic (January 1993), there were still many human rights abuses since the operation of the new constitution. The report of the GCHPR noted that the government still had a monopoly over the electronic media, which could potentially infringe on the right to free expression.

References: LaVerle Berry (ed.), *Ghana: A Country Study* (Washington, D.C.: Government Printing Office, 1995); Evelyn A. Ankumah, *The African Commission on Human Right and People's Rights: Practice and Procedures* (The Hague: Human Rights Commission, 1996).

GUINEAN HUMAN RIGHTS ORGANIZATION. (Guinea).

This nongovernmental human rights association is affiliated with the International Federation for Human Rights in Paris. Members of the organizations were arrested in November 1990 for demonstrations against the police.

Reference: US Department of State, *Country Reports on Human Rights Practices for 1993* (Washington, D.C.: Government Printing Office, 1994).

GUINEAN ORGANIZATION FOR THE DEFENSE OF HUMAN AND CITIZEN RIGHTS (OGDH). (Guinea).

In Guinea, family members and friends are responsible for feeding prisoners in the country's jails. The police brutality is common. The OGDH determined that prisoners in at least one major prison, located in N'zerekore, suffered more from neglect and lack of resources than from mistreatment. According the OGDH, the prison there was a converted grain warehouse built in 1932 for 72 prisoners, but then housed 120 inmates.

Reference: US Department of State, *Country Reports on Human Rights Practices for 1993* (Washington, D.C.: Government Printing Office, 1994).

H

HUMAN RIGHTS AFRICA (HRA). (Nigeria).

In 1995, the HRA chairman was Olatunji Abayomi, who was a prisoner of conscience. Long before the **CLO** began to report on the sad conditions of jails in Nigeria, the HRA approached the Attorney General of Nigeria asking for improved prison conditions. The Nigerian Minister claimed that the Babangida government would improve conditions, especially in the area of food and medical care. Organizers of the HRA resorted to a strategy of constructive engagement. It asked respected Nigerians to see the government ministers demanding the release of prisoners against whom no specific charges could be made. Relying on "common sense" and "reason" to prevail on the government, this group argued that the existing hate relationship between the government and human rights groups did not contribute to democratic development.

References: Eileen McCarthy-Arnolds et al., *Africa, Human Rights, and the Global System* (Westport, CT.: Greenwood Press, 1994); Abdullahi A. An-Na'im (ed.), *Human Rights in Cross-Cultural Perspectives: A Quest for Consensus* (Philadelphia: University of Pennsylvania Press, 1992); Claude E. Welch, *Protecting Human Rights in Africa* (Philadelphia: University of Pennsylvania Press, 1995).

HUMAN RIGHTS AND DISCOVERY. (Mozambique).

In December 1996, this relatively modest organization was formed with the stated objectives of promoting, protecting, and developing human rights.

Reference: US Department of State, *Country Reports on Human Rights Practices for 1993* (Washington, D.C.: Government Printing Office, 1994).

HUMAN RIGHTS ASSOCIATION OF SWAZILAND (HUMARAS). (Swaziland).

Although the government does not encourage human rights activities by domestic and international organizations, local organizations exist in Swaziland. The most prominent organization, the HUMARAS speaks out on human rights issues and works as a mediator in land and labor disputes.

Reference: US Department of State, *Country Reports on Human Rights Practices for 1993* (Washington, D.C.: Government Printing Office, 1994).

HUMAN RIGHTS CLINIC AND EDUCATION CENTER.
(Cameroon).

This organization holds seminars and workshops on various aspects of human rights and publishes reports of human rights violations.

Reference: US Department of State, *Country Reports on Human Rights Practices for 1993* (Washington, D.C.: Government Printing Office, 1994).

HUMAN RIGHTS COMMISSION (HRC). (South Africa).

National human rights commissions have mostly been ineffective simply because they have been financed by the national governments in Africa. The challenge that faced these national commissions was whether their actions would help to improve the government's respect for human rights in practice and bring relief to victims of abuse. South Africa's HRC showed the greatest signs of taking an active part in criticizing the government and actively pressing human rights concerns. In October 1997, it issued its first subpoena against a government department. Based in Johannesburg, this monitoring organization launched campaigns against detention, political trials, and restrictions on individuals. It makes its finding known through press releases, regular news reports, and information sheets. In 1994, it set up a small bureaucracy for the investigation of claims and the creation of reports on human rights. The commission also supports individuals who seek redress through the courts. Another important role of the commission is to scrutinize and propose legislation and issue reports to Parliament. Thus a major issue of rights may be raised in Parliament as well as in the courts. In 1992, this commission reported that 300 people were killed in internal violence and pressed for governmental intervention.

References: Paul. B. Rich (ed.), *Reaction and Renewal in South Africa* (New York: St. Martin's Press, 1996); Human Rights Internet, *Human Rights Internet: Reporter* (Boston, MA: Harvard Law School, February 1994); George M. Houser in *Africa Today* (4th quarter 1992).

HUMAN RIGHTS COMMITTEE OF SOUTH AFRICA. (South Africa).

The Human Rights Committee of South Africa, an NGO, monitors domestic violence and state repression, asking police officers what they would do with a complaint of rape. A spot survey conducted by the group found that 90 percent of the officers did not know what to do with a woman's complaint. This group works as a contact organization. The Durban office of the Human Rights Committee of South Africa has recorded a number of rapes apparently committed with a political motive. For example, four rapes were allegedly committed in the violence-torn northern part of Durban during June and July 1995. The group also reports on political violence.

Reference: Human Rights Watch, *Violence Against Women in South Africa* (New York: Human Rights Watch, 1995).

HUMAN RIGHTS COMMITTEE OF THE NIGERIAN BAR ASSOCIATION. (Nigeria).

This committee is concerned with selected types of rights violations in Nigeria.

Reference: US Department of State, *Country Reports on Human Rights Practices for 1993* (Washington, D.C.: Government Printing Office, 1994).

HUMAN RIGHTS DEFENCE ASSOCIATION (AZADHO).

(Democratic Republic of Congo, formerly Zaire).

This nongovernmental rights organization defends the human rights defenders and offers them concrete support in times of need. It claims that in 1998, the government stepped up its accusations and threats against human rights defenders and specifically targeted the AZADHO to incite hatred toward it. In March 1998, the president of the group, Guillaume Ngefa, argued that the government should put to trial those who had inflicted physical punishment on rights defenders. Recently, it called on the government of President Kabila to conform to the provisions of the Universal Declaration of Human Rights and to the regional and international instruments dealing with human rights with which the Democratic Republic of Congo had been associated.

Reference: The Human Rights Action Network, http://www. derechos.org/human-rights/actions/.

HUMAN RIGHTS DEFENCE GROUP. (Cameroon).

This NGO reports on torture and beatings of both political detainees and criminal suspects by the police. In April 1996, a journalist associated with the Human Rights Defence Group was arrested when he tried to stop a policeman from beating another person.

Reference: Amnesty International, USA, *Amnesty International Report, 1996* (New York: Amnesty International Publications, 1996).

HUMAN RIGHTS INFORMATION AND DOCUMENTATION SYSTEM (HURIDOCS). (France).

A nonprofit participatory international communications network founded in Strasbourg, France, in 1979, the HURIDOCS has since provided a worldwide clearinghouse for information on human rights. With concentration on developing documentation centers in several African countries, it has been engaged in developing agreed-upon terminology and standard formats for collecting and disseminating bibliographic entries of interest to human rights monitoring. It has direct impact on African human rights movements. Funded mostly by Norwegians and other Europeans, it was at one time chaired by a Ghanaian law professor. It trained Africans in the technical details of documenting international human rights standards, and it sought to establish a common foundation for documentation. Specifically, it held workshops in Kinshasa, Zaire in September 1991; Banjul, The Gambia in August, 1993; and in Nairobi, Kenya in October 1994. At times it gave special training to organizations such as the Civil Liberties Organization in Lagos, Nigeria and the Legal Resources Centre in Harare in Zimbabwe. It has not given open publicity of rights abuses. Its public forum is a periodical called *Huridocs News*.

References: Claude E. Welch, *Protecting Human Rights in Africa* (Philadelphia: University of Pennsylvania Press, 1995); Alex Schmid and Albert J. Jongman (eds.), *Monitoring Human Rights Violations* (Leiden, The Netherlands: Centre for the Study of Social Conflicts, 1992); Edward Lawson, *Encyclopedia of Human Rights* (New York: Taylor & Francis, 1991).

HUMAN RIGHTS LEAGUE. (Ethiopia).

Efforts to establish a human rights commission and ombudsman under the auspices of the Council of Peoples' Representatives have yet to produce tangible results in Ethiopia. In December 1996, a group of activists founded the Human Rights League, which was not given legal status by the government. Six of its board members were detained in November 1997. Two of the members were ill-treated while in police custody.

Reference: Human Rights Watch, *World Report 1998* (New York: Human Rights Watch, 1998).

HUMAN RIGHTS LEAGUE OF GUINEA-BISSAU (LDH).
(Guinea-Bissau).

Dozens of soldiers and civilians were detained and killed during the alleged plot to overthrow the government in March 1993. This NGO questioned the legality of detention of political opponents and argued that extractions of statements made before the military commission were broadcast on television, thereby prejudicing the rights of those accused to be presumed innocent until proved guilty. With 3,000 members in the country, this organization has been the leading organization for advancing human rights. It is funded by members' dues as well as contributions from foreign NGOs, and several countries, including Germany and Sweden. On several occasions, the LDH asked for access to prisoners in jail, but the government refused, arguing that the LDH was involved in a coup plot. Members of the LDH reported that there was occasional verbal harassment by police. The LDH's monitors estimated that 90 percent of the prison population were pretrial detainees arrested without warrants.

References: US Department of State, *Country Reports on Human Rights Practices for 1993* (Washington, D.C.: Government Printing Office, 1994); Amnesty International USA, *Amnesty International Report, 1994* (New York: Amnesty International, 1994).

HUMAN RIGHTS LEAGUE OF KATANGA. (Democratic Republic of Congo, formerly Zaire).

This organization is concerned with the waves of attacks on inhabitants of the Kasai region of Zaire. In 1993, its attorney Mbayabu Kanyama was arrested for assisting US reporters who were investigating political attacks. He fled from Lubumbashi and went to the capital, Kinshasa.

Reference: Lawyers Committee for Human Rights, *In Defense of Rights: Attacks on Lawyers and Judges in 1993* (New York: Lawyers Committee for Human Rights, 1993).

HUMAN RIGHTS MONITORS. (Nigeria).

This group of monitors is based in northern Nigeria. This association was founded by attorney John Matthew and Festus Okoyo. Matthew was arrested in June 1993 for distributing Civil Liberties literature calling for nonviolent protests over the cancellation of the June 1993 election. The group, in cooperation with the Civil Liberties Union, defends detainees in Nigeria.

Reference: Lawyers Committee for Human Rights, *In Defense of Rights* (New York: Lawyers Committee for Human Rights, 1994).

HUMAN RIGHTS NETWORK (HURINET). (Uganda).

This human rights network is an umbrella organization for nine large human rights organizations that are active in Uganda. It publishes a quarterly human rights newsletter.

Reference: US Department of State, *Country Reports on Human Rights Practices for 1993* (Washington, D.C.: Government Printing Office, 1994).

HUMAN RIGHTS STUDY CENTER. (Ghana).

This rights group of lawyers was created at the Law Faculty at the University of Ghana at Legon. The center issues leaflets to educate the general public about human rights.

Reference: US Department of State, *Country Reports on Human Rights Practices for 1993* (Washington, D.C.: Government Printing Office, 1994).

HUMAN RIGHTS TRUST (HRT). (South Africa).

This rights group was organized mainly by the clergy in South Africa to, among other things, trace the whereabouts of politically charged detainees, who were mostly blacks. Roy Riordan, a Port Elizabeth academic, headed the HRT in 1987. The group had its offices in the Eastern Cape. Two human rights advocates, Mrs. Euralia Banda and another person were engaged in extensive human rights monitoring in the Eastern Cape. On March 21, 1985, 29 black people were killed by the security police during a peaceful march from the black township of Langa to the white part of the town to protest the removal of the township. Mrs. Banda and her associate collected evidence to bring a legal case against the police. Mrs. Banda's husband, Emson, a political activist, was detained without a trial for over a year from 1986 to 1987.

Reference: Human Rights Watch / Africa Watch, *No Neutral Ground: South Africa's Confrontation with the Activist Churches* (New York, Human Rights Watch: 1989).

HUMAN RIGHTS WATCH/AFRICA (HRW). (USA).

Human Rights Watch began in 1978 with the founding of its European division, Helsinki Watch. Today, it has five divisions including the African division. Based in New York, the HRW/Africa has produced consistent quality results. HRW claims to speak on behalf of "global" or universal human rights. Some questioned HWR's strong stance against weakening its commitment to universal standards by recognizing "weak" cultural relativism. Abdullahi An-Na'im, an African, was Executive Director of Human Rights Watch between 1993 and 1995. In a major study, "Indivisible Human" in September 1992, the HRW argued that many economic and cultural privations such as famine and abuse of workers' rights arose from political conditions. The HRW/Africa has thematic projects on arms transfers, children's rights, and women's rights besides its preoccupation with civil and political rights in African countries. It publishes its reports in an impartial way.

References: US Department of State, *Country Reports on Human Rights Practices for 1993* (Washington, D.C.: Government Printing Office, 1994); Abdullahi A. An-Na'im, *Human Rights in Cross-Cultural Perspectives: A Quest for Consensus* (Philadelphia: University of Pennsylvania Press, 1992). Claude E. Welch, *Protecting Human Rights in Africa* (Philadelphia: University of Pennsylvania Press, 1995).

IFE COLLECTIVE. (Nigeria).

There was political repression in Nigeria in the wake of structural adjustment program (SAP), and this group of radicals based at Ile-Ife argued that people had the right of resistance against hunger, unemployment, and socio-economic injustice in Nigeria.

Reference: Eileen McCarthy-Arnolds et al., *Africa, Human Rights, and the Global System* (Westport, CT: Greenwood Press, 1994).

INSTITUTE FOR HUMAN RIGHTS EDUCATION. (Senegal).

Formed in Dakar, Senegal in 1979, the institute received financial support from UNESCO, but it is still struggling to develop structure, resources, and programs under the aegis of the **Inter-African Union of Lawyers.**

References: Harry M. Scoble, "Human Rights Non-Governmental Organization in Black Africa," in Claude E. Welch, *Human Rights and Development in Africa* (Albany, NY: State University of New York Press, 1987).

INTER-AFRICA NETWORK FOR HUMAN RIGHTS AND DEVELOPMENT (AFRONET). (Zambia).

The government of President Chiluba has been critical of the national origins of NGOs and foreign support for them. Along with other NGOs, this group monitored elections in 1996 and as such the Zambian government harassed some members of the group. The AFRONET took the brunt of state intolerance for expressing the view that the elections were not free or fair. The police raided the offices of the AFRONET, seizing files and documents.

Reference: Human Rights Watch, *World Report 1998* (New York: Human Rights Watch, 1998).

INTER-AFRICAN UNION OF HUMAN RIGHTS (UIDH). (French-speaking Africa).

The UIDH brought together human rights NGOs from Benin, Burkina Faso, Cameroon, the Central African Republic, Togo, Chad, and Burundi. It defined itself as "a common watchdog, on the African level, of the principles stated in the Universal Declaration of Human Rights and for the African Charter of Human and Peoples' Rights." Anglophone Africa did not show any interest in the union.

Reference: Akwasi Aidoo, "Africa: Democracy Without Human Rights," *Human Rights Quarterly* 15: (1993), 703-715.

INTER-AFRICAN UNION OF LAWYERS. (Senegal).

This group of lawyers created a nongovernmental commission on human rights.

References: Harry M. Scoble, "Human Rights Non-Governmental Organizations in Black Africa" in Claude E. Welch, Jr., and Ronald I. Meltzer (eds.), *Human Rights and Development in Africa* (Albany: State University of New York Press, 1984).

INTERNATIONAL COMMISSION OF JURISTS (ICJ). (Switzerland).

This commission was created 1952. Its mandate has been broadly defined as promoting the rule of law and the legal protection of human rights. Headquartered in Geneva, it has 75 sections throughout the world. This international legal organization has become an active proponent of strengthening the African Commission on Human and Peoples' Rights. In 1961, it convened the first all African Conference of Jurists at Lagos. That Conference recommended for the first time the adoption by the African governments of an African Convention of Human Rights. This proposal was further developed in Dakar in 1967. In November 1989, the ICJ held a seminar in Banjul, The Gambia, declaring that a center — the

African Centre for Democracy and Human Rights Studies — be established to support and promote human rights in Africa. In February 1990, another seminar was organized in Harare, Zimbabwe. There, Prime Minister Robert Mugabe gave a new orientation in thinking when he declared that there was the existence of "the universality of Human Rights a principle which Zimbabwe cherishes." In 1993, an African commission in Senegal, organized by ICJ, recommended that an All African Court of Human and Peoples' Rights be established along with some regional courts. In 1993, the ICJ jurists prepared a draft for the African international court. It is still hoped that the concept of Human Rights Court for Africa may soon become a reality. Moreover, the ICJ spent money and time in bringing 65 groups (from 1991 to 1994) to African Commission sessions and premeeting workshops. The ICJ wants to make the reporting process a significant opportunity for constructive dialogue between states parties and individual Commissioners, and between the African Commissioners and NGO representatives. Advocacy to stop abuses relies mostly on legal skills. The ICJ has prepared a sort of "barefoot lawyers" in Africa to spread legal procedure and help develop foundations for civil society.

References: Raymond Sock, "The Case for an African Court of Human and Peoples Rights," *African Topics* (March-April 1994); Claude E. Welch, *Protecting Human Rights in Africa* (Philadelphia: University of Pennsylvania Press, 1995); International Commission of Jurists, *Paralegals in Rural Africa* (Geneva, Switzerland: International Commission of Jurists, 1991).

INTERNATIONAL FEDERATION OF WOMEN LAWYERS.
(Lesotho).

This local chapter of the International Federation of Women Lawyers has taken a leading role in educating women regarding their rights under customary and common law. It highlights the importance of women participating in the democratic process.

Reference: US State Department, *Country Reports on Human Rights Practices for 1993* (Washington, D.C.: Government Printing Office, 1994).

ITEKA. (Burundi).

Ethnic violence between Tutsi (14 percent of the people) and Hutu (85 percent) erupted in October 1991. Soldiers killed the first democratically elected President, Melchior Ndadaye, a Hutu, who had defeated Buyoya in presidential elections. The assassination of President Ndadaye led to a massive outflow of refugees from Burundi. Both Tutsi and Hutu engaged in massive revenge killings of civilians. Since the assassination of President Ndadaye, there were massive human rights violations by all sides. Under the Buyoya government, the two independent groups — ITEKA and SONERA — faced bureaucratic obstacles, such as inordinate delays by Ministry of Justice officials in response to requests for information on specific cases or permission to visit prisons. However, these two groups investigated and reported individual cases of human rights violations on many occasions.

Reference: US State Department, *Country Reports on Human Rights Practices for 1993* (Washington, D.C.: Government Printing Office, 1994).

IVORIAN ASSOCIATION FOR THE PROMOTION OF HUMAN RIGHTS. (Ivory Coast).

This group was established in 1991 for the purpose of improving Ivorians' awareness of their basic rights.

Reference: US Department of State, *Country Reports on Human Rights Practices for 1993* (Washington, D.C.: Government Printing Office, 1994).

IVORIAN LEAGUE OF HUMAN RIGHTS (LIDHO). (Ivory Coast).

Formed in 1987 and recognized by the government in July 1990, the LIDHO has actively investigated alleged violations of human rights and issued reports critical of the government's human rights record. Houphouet-Boigny's 33-year oppressive rule ended with his death in 1990, but his legacy continued as his designated successor, Henry K. Bedie, became president. There were no known political killings by government security forces in 1993. However, the "antivandal" law passed by the National Assembly in 1992 was designed to punish political opponents. The LIDHO criticized the law as being unduly vague and for imposing collective punishment for the crimes of a few. There has been some discrimination against the leaders of the group. For example, Professor Degny Segui, the head of the LIDHO, was denied permission to attend the World Conference on Human Rights in Vienna. He was also forbidden to travel to Strasbourg to teach courses at the Institute for Human Rights. The group reported that prison guards were occasionally raping female prisoners, and complained that military officials responsible for human rights violations were not persecuted.

References: US Department of State, *Country Reports on Human Rights Practices for 1993* (Washington, D.C.: Government Printing Office, 1994); Lawyers Committee for Human Rights, *In Defense of Rights: Attacks on Lawyers and Judges in 1993* (New York: Lawyers Committee for Human Rights, 1993).

J

JOURNALISTS SANS FRONTIERES. (Rwanda).

Rwanda has nine human rights organizations, five were formed in 1990 and 1991, and four were formed in 1993. This journalists' group reports on political killings and ethnic violence committed on diverse groups. They publish findings without much governmental interference.

Reference: US Department of State, *Country Reports on Human Rights Practices for 1996* (Washington, D.C.: Government Printing Office, 1997).

JUSTICE AND PEACE COMMISSIONS OF THE CATHOLIC CHURCH. (Democratic Republic of Congo, formerly Zaire).

Since 1990, this prodemocracy and human rights NGO has been able to function in Zaire in a manner that was inconceivable during the twenty-five years of a one-party state. In many regions, the first human rights associations emerged from the churches, and this group was one of them. It has developed a grassroots structure modeled on the parishes and is able to organize the population at neighborhood levels to confront such problems as public security.

Reference: Human Rights Watch, *Zaire* (New York, Human Rights Watch: 1997).

K

KENYA ALLIANCE FOR THE ADVANCEMENT OF CHILDREN (KAAC). (Kenya).

This private association assists street children in filing preliminary complaints with the police for misconduct and mistreatment of children by Kenyan police. But the group itself has not commenced private actions against police atrocities. In 1995, children's courts committed many children under 18 years of age to children's homes and remand prisons. The KAAC argued that disciplinary matters should be separated from protection matters. The KAAC complained that when a child begged he was taken unduly to the remand home, which meant that the child was being disciplined by the police and not protected.

Reference: Human Rights Watch, *Juvenile Injustice: Police Abuse and Detention of Street Children in Kenya* (New York, Human Rights Watch, 1997).

KENYA HUMAN RIGHTS COMMISSION (KHRC). (Kenya).

Despite obstructions created by President Moi's government's repressive measures, Kenyans formed several vibrant and thriving human rights groups. This well-organized nongovernmental commission, which shares premises with the **Kituo Cha Sheria** (a free legal aid center), reported that in the first few months of 1996, the police killed 88 people for political reasons, and in the same year 17 detainees died as a result of police torture. The group claimed that some of those killed were children and innocent bystanders. In a particularly well-documented case, the KHRC published medical reports for the cases of Virginia N. Wambui and Bernard M. Kariki, who were detained by police in December 1995. The medical reports confirmed that they were kicked and whipped by police. This organization found out that in 1994 children prisoners were kept in miserable conditions in Industrial Areas in Nairobi, Shimolatewa (Mombassa), Kodiaga (Kisumu), and Langate women's prison (Nairobi). According to its estimates, there were 583 deaths in Nairobi Industrial Remand Prison in four years. Children slept on the floor without mattresses, and boys went without food for days.

References: Kenya Human Rights Commission Prisons Project, *A Death Sentence: Prison Conditions in Kenya* (Nairobi, Kenya: Kenya Human Rights Commission, 1994); US Department of State, *Country Reports on Human Rights Practices for 1993* (Washington, D.C.: Government Printing Press, 1994).

KENYA PUBLIC LAW INSTITUTE (KPLI). (Kenya).

The KPLI was founded with the help of the International Commission of Jurists national section in Kenya. Its primary support came from two organizations: the National Christian Council of Kenya and the Law Society of Kenya. The Institute has both a human rights mandate as well as a legal aid and advice mandate. Under its leadership, the first mobile clinic for legal aid and legal information was started in June 1986. It used paralegals in the rural clinic and toward the end of the decade introduced training programs for interested people. The reform program was drawn heavily from the successful experience in India where legal aid was free. The Institute's priority is human rights and it publicizes human rights violations.

References: International Commission of Jurists, *Human and Peoples' Rights in Africa and the African Charter* (Geneva, Switzerland: International Commission of Jurists, 1986); US Department of State, *Country Reports on Human Rights Practices for 1996* (Washington, D.C.: Government Printing Office, 1997).

KENYA SOCIAL CONGRESS PARTY. (Kenya).

This opposition party maintains comprehensive files on

human rights abuses, carefully tracking extra-judicial violence and disruption of opposition political meetings. This party published a detailed study of human rights violations committed in a district in Nyanza province in Kenya.

Reference: US Department of State, *Country Reports on Human Rights Practices for 1996* (Washington, D.C.: Government Printing Office, 1997).

KITUO CHA SHERIA. (Kenya).

Originally this group was known as Kituo Cha Mashauri, which means " legal help" in Swahili. It started its operation in 1973. In the beginning, it was purely a volunteer organization of lawyers and law students. In 1985, it engaged a skilled attorney. This free legal aid center shares premises with the **Kenya Human Rights Commission**. Sheria operates in Kenya on a modest scale but with impressive objectives. It provided free legal aid in civil and noncapital crimes in Kenya, because the government offered legal aid as a rule only in capital cases. Currently, its goal is to promote rights through community outreach and training programs. The Kenyan police view the group with suspicion and disdain, and they claim that in the first three months of 1995, Kituo Cha Sheria bombed six times.

References: Gathii Irungu, "Twenty Years Caring for Justice," *Haki Mail* (quarterly journal of the Kituo Cha Sheria, 1: 1 [April 1993]); Claude E. Welch, *Protecting Human Rights in Africa* (Philadelphia: University of Pennsylvania Press, 1995); http://www.derechos.org /human-rights.afr/kenya-1.html.

KULAYA CENTER FOR VICTIMS OF DOMESTIC VIOLENCE. (Mozambique).

In 1996, a group of NGOs active in the women's rights area established the Kulaya Center for Victims of Domestic Violence. The Center, which operates out of the Maputo central hospital, currently has about 15 beds and relies on foreign funding. The Center urges women, who are victims of domestic violence, to press charges.

Reference: US Department of State, *Country Reports on Human Rights Practices for 1993* (Washington, D.C.: Government Printing Office, 1994).

L

LAND CENTER FOR HUMAN RIGHTS (LCHR). (Egypt).

This independent Cairo-based rights group documented how security forces intervened to prevent conferences and meetings that were popular farmers' mechanisms to discuss concern about a new law regarding farming lands. The Law No 96 of 1992 lifted rent control and protection against eviction. When farmers protested the law, police harassed them. The group argued that the farmers' protests were part of freedom of expression and as such their rights should not have been abridged.

Reference: Human Rights Watch, *World Report 1998* (New York: Human Rights Watch, 1998).

LAW ASSOCIATION OF ZAMBIA (LAZ). (Zambia).

This legally constituted lawyers' association in Zambia has set up a Human Rights Committee to promote civic education. It conducts seminars on human rights in all provincial capitals. As a major human rights sector, the LAZ has received several reports on police violence and prison conditions. According to the group, conditions in Zambian prisons were harsh and life threatening. The group reported that three prisoners at Singogo Remand Prison in Ndola died within a six-week period in July and August 1993. At the instance of this rights group, the Ndola Magistrate ordered the release on bail of prisoners awaiting trial. The LAZ petitioned the Home

Ministry in Lusaka to permit access to prison cells, but the government denied the request.

References: Swedish NGO Foundation of Human Rights, *The Status of Human Rights Organizations in Sub-Saharan Africa* (Stockholm: The International Human Rights Internship Program Publications, 1994); US State Department, *Country Reports on Human Rights Practices for 1993* (Washington, D.C.: Government Printing Office, 1994).

LAW SOCIETY OF KENYA (LSK). (Kenya).

This statutory body was created by the Law Society of Kenya Act, passed by the legislative assembly in Kenya. At first, this bar association was concerned more with narrow matters, such as the maintenance of the fee structure for lawyers, than with standing up for individual rights. Increasingly, it began to criticize the flaws in judicial administration. The government courts severely restricted the LSK's ability to speak out freely on matters relating to the administration of justice and to democratic institutions. Nevertheless, the organization focused on several themes. First, it commented publicly on the subject of justice in Kenya. It argued that the government potentially had the sole right to decide who could or could not practice law in the country — a responsibility that traditionally belonged to the Council of the LSK. Second, the Society led the renewed demands on President Moi to end the one-party state. In 1991, the association urged the government to repeal the Prevention of Public Safety Act, which curtailed freedom of assembly and speech. Moreover, political prisoners, the group claimed, were treated badly by the police. Third, the LSK complained that President Moi and his party, KANU, had failed to prevent ethnic violence. With the help of other human rights organizations, such as **International Commission of Jurists** (Kenya), the LSK organized a seminar in May 1992 to determine a course of action against the government's violation of political rights. In its report, the society stated that the police attacks were organized under a central command, often in the presence of local administrative and security officers. The report concluded that the violence had resulted in the displacement of 50,000 people. The LSK, which has been in the forefront of the defense of rights and the rule of law, is now publicly accused by President Moi of "serving the interests of foreigners."

References: Africa Watch, *Divide and Rule (Kenya)* (New York: Human Rights Watch, 1993); Drews S. Days et al., *Justice Enjoined: The State of the Judiciary in Kenya* (New York: Robert Kennedy Memorial Center for Human Rights, 1992).

LAWYERS' COMMITTEE FOR HUMAN RIGHTS (LCHR).
(Democratic Republic of Congo, formerly Zaire).

The African Commission wanted to visit Zaire to verify allegations of violations of rights, but there was no response from the government of Zaire in 1994. The LCHR has occasionally reported human rights violations in Zaire to the African Commission.

Reference: U. O. Umozurike, *Self-Determination in International Law* (Hamden, CT: Archon, 1972); U. O. Umozurike, "The Protection of Human Rights Under the Banjul African Charter on Human and Peoples' Rights," *African Journal of International Law* 1 (1988), 65-83

LAWYERS' COMMITTEE FOR HUMAN RIGHTS. (Kenya).

This group argues that the government in a liberal democracy should not have the right to harass editors and censor the press. This committee reported that in the early 1990s the Moi government, using the penal code, banned newspapers, which this group considered a violation of civil rights.

Reference: Lawyers Committee for Human Rights, *Kenya* (New York: Lawyers Committee for Human Rights, 1994).

LAWYERS FOR HUMAN RIGHTS (LHR). (South Africa).

This leading organization, based in Pretoria, fights prejudice and discrimination in the areas of race, gender, ethnic origin, color, religion, culture, and language. During the 1994 general election, it argued that blind voters should be able to cast a secret ballot. Established in 1979, the LHR identifies with the international human rights groups by attending conferences. Currently, it has 18 regional offices operating throughout South Africa. They are staffed by competent paralegals who work in conjunction with a Regional Director. The LHR organizes "The Human Rights Education Project," which is centered on a Human Rights work-book titled "Human Rights for All." The work-book follows the Street Law format and is accompanied by a Teachers Manual. One chapter of the book deals with fair procedures after arrest, and it covers such issues as: whether human rights should ever be limited in the interests of national security and the death penalty. The LHR's projects are varied. One project is called "The Human Rights Education Project," which is expected to play a valuable role in ensuring that South African youths understand how human rights can be protected in the criminal justice system in a democratic and nonracial society. In 1991, the LHR established a disability rights unit, which has intervened in 50 legal cases and represented less formally many disabled people in their dealings with the bureaucracy. The majority of these cases relate to arbitrary discriminations of ineligibility because of physical disability. This group acts as a contact group for the victims. One of its publications is *Rights*.

References: M. Cheri Bassiouni and Ziyad Motala (eds.), *The Protection of Human Rights in African Criminal Proceedings* (London: Martinus Publishers, 1995); David McQuoid-Masos et al., *Human Rights for All* (Pretoria, South Africa: David Philip Publishers, 1991).

LAWYERS FOR HUMAN RIGHTS IN PIETERMARITZBURG.
(South Africa).

In 1992, this private contact group ran a Juvenile Justice Project, with one lawyer and one paralegal. Every child in magistrate's court in the area was contacted, and efforts were made to contact parents. As a result, children spent less times in custody.

Reference: Africa Watch, *Prison Conditions in South Africa* (New York: Human Rights Watch, 1994).

LEAGUE FOR THE PROMOTION OF HUMAN RIGHTS IN TOGO (LPDH). (Togo).

With lawyers, teachers, and high-ranking government servants as its members, and supported by a paid staff, this group has organized several conferences on rights issues. It believes that violations are perpetrated by both the government and the opposition, and thus both abuses should be reported.

Reference: Swedish NGO Foundation, *The Status of Human Rights Organizations in Sub-Saharan Africa* (Stockholm: The International Human Rights Internship Program Publications, 1994).

LEAGUE OF HUMAN RIGHTS AND DEMOCRACY. (Sierra Leone).

Local human rights groups are allowed to operate in Sierra Leone. The League of Human Rights and Democracy, a private organization, monitors all human rights issues, but it concentrates on issues related to press freedom and conditions of prisoners. Its effectiveness is hampered by government intimidation and lack of resources. In at least one case in 1993, the League's director was summoned by the police for his activities.

Reference: US Department of State, *Country Reports on Human Rights Practices for 1993* (Washington, D.C.: Government Printing Office, 1994).

LEAGUE OF KENYA WOMEN VOTERS. (Kenya).
This women's self-help group has asked for equality, development, and human rights. It claimed that in June 1993, armed police beat women attending a seminar organized by the League of Kenya Women Voters. It also argues that the government of President Moi does not investigate and punish officers who are involved with human rights abuses in Kenya. This women's group has been under constant attack by the government.

Reference: Human Rights: Kenya, http://wwww.derechos.org/human-rights/afr/kenya-l.html

LEAGUE OF TUNISIA FOR HUMAN RIGHTS (LTDH). (Tunisia).
In the 1970s and 1980s, North Africa saw the proliferation of indigenous human rights groups, which changed the dynamics of the political scene in autocratic regimes that were supported by religious orthodoxy. The LTDH was the foremost of these groups. Founded in 1977, the League enlisted support not only from the activists, but also from the influential members of the Tunisian government under President Ben Ali. Ben Ali hoped to woo the League's activists for political reasons. Naturally, a question was raised: Did the LTDH influence President Ben Ali and move him into new directions for political reforms, or did he simply use it for political gains? It is difficult to distinguish the League's impact on the formal political discourse in the post-Bourguiba era. In Tunisia, the effectiveness of the LTDH was weakened early in 1991 by internal disputes about the Gulf War. But the organization since then has refocused on serious human rights issues, such

as political arrests, torture, and repression. In the midst of serious reprisals during the final months of Habib Bourguiba's rule, the LTDH achieved some success in highlighting human rights abuses. The Tunisian regime has tacitly acknowledged at least the rhetorical importance of human rights by creating an official council of its own to deal with human rights issues.

Reference: Susan Waltz, "Making Waves: The Political Impact of Human Rights Groups in North Africa," *Journal of Modern African Studies*, 29: 3 (1991): 481-504.

LEGAL ASSISTANCE CENTRE (LAC). (Namibia).

The LAC began in 1988 in Windhoek, the capital. Its activities included human rights, labor mistreatment, and education. The LAC developed programs for the poor, who were abused by the government. Its founder was Advocate David Smuts, a Harvard educated elite based in Windhoek. His long battle within the legal system of Namibia prepared the way for a post-independence respect for the rule of law. He challenged the white apartheid government's basic discriminatory legal structures in the 1980s. He was in touch with American civil rights leaders. Although most of his cases against the government were dismissed by the white judges, he won a case in 1988. The LAC handled Supreme Court applications for workers, mostly blacks, who were forcibly removed from their living quarters by the police after the black workers were dismissed from their jobs. It represented the families of mine workers after the mine disaster in November 1988. The same year, it organized a training seminar for trade union officials. It claimed that the likelihood of success against the government was small because the Roman-Dutch legal heritage of South Africa gave great discretion to the state. Currently, the LAC operates freely, criticizing the government's handling of the SWAPO's detainee issue, the treatment of refugees, and misconduct by members of the police and defense forces. The LAC focuses not only on legal education but also on women's rights. It works with the Ministry of Education and Culture to develop a constitutional curriculum for schools.

References: Claude E. Welch, *Protecting Human Rights in Africa* (Philadelphia: University of Pennsylvania Press, 1995); Raoul Wallenberg Institute, *Human Rights Workshop Namibia* (Lund: The

Institute, February 1991); US Department of State, *Country Reports on Human Rights Practices for 1993* (Washington, D.C.: Government Printing Office, 1994).

LEGAL EDUCATION ACTION PROJECT (LEAP). (South Africa). This NGO is concerned with human rights education. It has made some progress toward training paralegals who are expected to educate the people in the rural communities in South Africa on their legal and human rights issues. Here emphasis has been placed on reaching communities through their local vernacular languages.

Reference: Brendalyn P. Ambrose, *Democratization and the Protection of Human Rights in Africa: Problems and Prospects* (Westport, CT: Praeger, 1995).

LEGAL RESEARCH AND RESOURCES DEVELOPMENT CENTRE IN NIGERIA (LRRDC). (Nigeria). The LRRDC often focuses on illiterate and poor persons with limited formal schooling. Its members have skills essential for protecting human rights through the courts. They try to develop a culture of human rights that links knowledge about issues to awareness of possible solutions. One of its leaders was Tokunbo Ige who studied constitutional law at the University of Lagos in the mid-1980s and human rights law at the University of Essex. The LRRDC has turned to training paralegals. By 1994, it had prepared 43 women and men to assist persons in the mid-western Nigerian city of Benin and in the southwestern town of Ijebu as assistants. It has set up clinics in ideal places. It tailors programs to the specific needs of numerically large but politically insignificant citizens.

References: Claude E. Welch, *Protecting Human Rights in Africa* (Philadelphia: University of Pennsylvania Press, 1995); Amy S. Tsanga and Olatokunbo Ige, *A Paralegal Trainer's Manual for Africa* (Geneva: International Commission of Jurists, 1994).

LEGAL RESOURCES CENTRE (LRC). (South Africa). In 1979, this Johannesburg-based LRC began operation to provide legal services to the poor. It was particularly concerned with cases relating to the exploitation of workers and abuses of power by public officials. It determined that restricted to 13 percent of the land in South Africa, black people in all provinces were at the mercy of a legal system that denied them fundamental rights. Because the state run Legal Aid did not do much, South Africa's first private /public interest law firm was created at the instance of the LRC. Since 1994, it has been helping the poor in legal matters in rural areas. Now it is responsible for the generation of a broad consciousness of the possibilities of "legal rights," which may not always be compatible with popular justice. The LRC litigated on behalf of the British community (7,000 strong), resisting attempts by the government to remove the community. Each of the regional LRC offices serves a network of Advice Offices, and each operates independently of the LRC. Directly, the LRC takes on cases referred to it by the Advice Offices that are beyond the competence of Advice Office workers. Indirectly, the LRC trains and supports community-based advice offices and collaborates with other organizations interested in promoting paralegal work. At an early stage, the LRC realized that because of the paucity of lawyers in the public interest arena, a great part of this very crucial work would have to done by paralegals in Advice Offices. These are based in communities with the LRC itself acting as a catalyst toward a greater rights consciousness and assertion of those rights to develop a working relationship with these structures wherever it operates. Recently, the LRC in Natal has been involved in monitoring meetings and rallies of protesters; in ongoing meetings with the Commissioner of the South African and Kwa Zulu Police and army to discuss problems and allegations made to the LRC by clients and their organizations; and in civil actions for damages arising out of security force actions. This legal center is determined to break up the old set of legal practices.

References: Paul. B. Rich (ed.), *Reaction and Renewal in South Africa* (New York: St. Martin's Press, 1996); International Commission of Jurists, *Paralegals in Rural Africa* (Geneva, Switzerland: International Commission of Jurists, 1991); Wallace Mgoqi, "The Work of the Legal Resource Centre in South Africa in the Area of Human Rights Promotion and Protection," *Journal of African Law* 36 (36), 1992, 1-10.

LEGAL RESOURCES FOUNDATION (LRF). (Zimbabwe).
In 1993, this group worked on the design of a legal and human rights syllabus to be incorporated into the recruits' training

curriculum. The LRF also conducted human rights training workshops for senior police officers and planned to conduct similar workshops for the police rank and file in 1994. In addition, it managed workshops for community relations officers for dealing with the mistreatment of women.

Reference: US Department of State, *Country Report on Human Rights Practices for 1993* (Washington, D.C.: Government Printing Office, 1994).

LEMBA WOMEN. (Democratic Republic of Congo, formerly Zaire). This women's organization is engaged in upholding women's rights as foremost rights. Lemba Women in Zaire are traditionally conscious of nutritional values of foods. They decide not only what to grow but also what to consume. Lemba Women set aside choice food items and sauces for their own and their children's consumption before feeding the men. According to this group, women's rights should get preference in the society.

Reference: Sandra W. Meditz (ed.), *Zaire: A Country Study* (Washington, D.C.: Government Printing Office, 1994).

LIBYAN HUMAN RIGHTS COMMISSION (LHRC). (Libya). Libya hardly has any effective rights group. This nonpolitical organization was established in 1985. It urged the Libyan government to comply with the rights provisions and principles that had been proclaimed in the **Universal Declaration of Human Rights, Amnesty International** and other rights associations.

Reference: Human Rights Internet, *Human Rights Internet: Reporter* (Boston, MA: Harvard Law School, February 1994).

M

MAENDELEO YA WANAWAKE ORGANIZATION (MYWO).
(Kenya).

This is one of the sixty or so NGOs dealing with rights issues in Kenya. Founded in 1952, it is the largest such group in Kenya in terms of both membership and number of women groups affiliated to it. Its main charge is to organize rural women for productive work. Earlier, many Kenyan women joined this organization, mainly to escape the harsh forced labor conditions that had been imposed by the British colonial government and big farmers. In 1985, it was divided into 800 women's groups. During the 1985 Nairobi Conference on Women, the MYWO assumed the leadership position in expressing women's rights, and the government supported its stance. In May 1987, it merged with the ruling party, KANU. Since then, it is not clear whether the new KANU/MYWO combination has lost its NGO status. Currently, the MYWO lays emphasis on the role of women as homemakers. Under a political marriage, the MYWO is unlikely to challenge those aspects of Kenyan legislation and political structure that are oppressive to women.

Reference: Maria Nzomo, "The Impact of the Women's Decade on Policies, Programs and Empowerment of Women in Kenya," *Issue* (Summer 1989): 9-17.

MALIAN ASSOCIATION FOR HUMAN RIGHTS (AMDH).
(Mali).

Mali has a constitutional government headed by President Alpha Conrare. In 1992, the Malians changed their government through free elections. There are two independent human rights organizations in the country, the AMDH and the smaller Malian League of Human Rights. Neither has been active in highlighting human rights abuses since the installation of democracy in Mali.

Reference: US Department of State, *Country Reports on Human Rights Practices for 1993* (Washington, D.C.: Government Printing Office, 1994).

MARIADI FABRICS. (Kenya).

This organization was started by American women living in Kenya to empower poor Kenyan women. It employed African women and girls in cottage industries. The women worked at a craft that drew on traditional African culture and yet was adapted to modern markets. Most of the designs came from African women, who themselves regarded the organization as an empowerment group.

Reference: Sue Ellen M. Charlton, *Women in Third World Development* (Boulder, CO: Westview Press, 1984).

MAURITANIAN HUMAN RIGHTS ASSOCIATION (AMDH).
(Mauritania).

This organization applied for recognition in 1991, but the government of Mauritania has accorded no permit. The AMDH was particularly concerned with the human rights abuses of the 1989-91 period. It has been very active in promoting its agenda, specifically in providing information to the press and in sponsoring educative seminars. Currently, the government does not cooperate with the group because it is fearful of any opposition voice. The AMDH is not affiliated with the opposition, but it has many opposition members. It has been more critical of the governmental abuses of political rights than the older organization, **Mauritanian League for Human Rights**.

Reference: US Department of State, *Country Reports on Human Rights Practices for 1993* (Washington, D.C.: Government Printing Office, 1994).

MAURITANIAN LEAGUE FOR HUMAN RIGHTS (MHRL).
(Mauritania).

The MHRL is the only human rights organization, which was founded in 1988, that was officially recognized by the government of President Taya. The 1992 multiparty election of a civilian president ended 14 years of military rule, but the military still had a very strong base within the administration. The MHRL organized the first Maghreb Conference on Human Rights. It tried then to probe the limits of political tolerance in the area of human rights. In 1989, it helped the emergence of a human rights institute in Tunis. It is not as critical of the governmental rights abuses of the 1989-91 period as the newer organization, **Mauritanian Human Rights Association**.

References: Jack Donnelly, *International Human Rights* (Boulder: Westview Press, 1993); US Department of State, *Country Reports on Human Rights Practices for 1993* (Washington, D.C.: Government Printing Office, 1994).

MEDIA RIGHTS AGENDA (MRA). (Nigeria).

This association brings to the notice of the **African Commission** many instances of violations of rights regarding dissemination of information, which is crucial, according to the Agenda, for a democratic society. In 1993, Nigerian authorities adopted a decree that required the compulsory registration of every newspaper and magazine. The registration fee itself was very high. Many newspapers were banned. The decree stipulated that it could not be challenged in court. The MRA protested these infringements. It reported cases of gross violations of press rights to the African Commission.

Reference: Evelyn A. Ankumah, *The African Commission on Human and Peoples' Rights: Practice and Procedures* (The Hague: Human Rights Commission, 1996).

MIGBE AYA (We Reject Poverty). (Benin).

This farmers union is concerned with the plight of the prisoners of conscience in Benin. In 1992, some of its members were detained by the security forces because they gave advice to an individual wanting to lodge a complaint

about an armed robbery in which police officers were
implicated.

Reference: Amnesty International USA, *Amnesty International Report*
(New York: Amnesty International Publications, 1994).

MILIMA. (Democratic Republic of Congo, formerly Zaire).

Faction groups, supported by the militia and Zairian soldiers,
killed thousands of Hutu and Tutsi refugees. The MILIMA, a
development and human rights NGO in Zaire working among
the Banyamulenge, had contact with the outside world to
report about killings by soldiers and militias. In August 1996,
the commissioner for Uvire Zone banned the MILIMA and
issued an arrest warrant for its president, apparently because
he had contacted journalists and representatives of the Carter
Center of Atlanta, Georgia, regarding human rights abuses
against the Banyamulenge.

Reference: Human Rights Watch, *Zaire* (New York: Human Rights
Watch, 1997).

MOROCCAN ASSOCIATION OF HUMAN RIGHTS (AMDH).
(Morocco).

The AMDH was set up in August 1979 by a small group of
dissidents, intellectuals, and lawyers at a time when a larger
group of dissidents (Frontistes) gained attention at home and
abroad. Its voice became weaker after 1983. When the USFP,
the mainstream party, became more popular, the AMDH's
supporters were increasingly isolated. It defends those rights
that are contained in the **Universal Declaration of Human
Rights**. It believes that world public opinion is the most
important lever for encouraging governments to respect the
human rights of their citizens.

References: Human Rights Internet, *Human Rights Internet: Reporter*
(Boston, MA: Harvard Law School, February 1994); Susan Waltz,
"Making Waves: The Political Impact of Human Rights Groups in North
Africa," *Journal of Modern African Studies* 29(3), 1991:481-504.

**MOROCCAN LEAGUE FOR DEFENSE OF HUMAN RIGHTS
(LMDDH).** (Morocco).

In 1972, a conservative nationalist party (Istiqlal) formed this
group. The LMDDH took the charge to promote respect for
human rights through publicity. It denounced injustice toward

Palestinians but it has never been outspoken.

Reference: Susan Waltz, "Making Waves: The Political Impact of Human Rights Groups in North Africa," *Journal of Modern African Studies* 29 (3), 1991: 481-504.

MOROCCAN ORGANIZATION FOR HUMAN RIGHTS (OMDH). (Morocco).

The Moroccan social order has been based on Moroccan conceptions of Islam in which God's will set the parameter of human action. Personal ties in this setting are generally more reliable than formal ideology. Against this "practical" ideology, the OMDH takes care of human rights problem. In 1988, a preparatory committee of forty scholars drafted the charter of the OMDH. At its Agdal meeting, the OMDH was officially born with the blessings of King Hassan II. The OMDH had a 19-member executive bureau. The bureau, comprising mostly political independents, was headed by Omar Azziman, a law professor who had no affiliation with any party. In 1989, the OMDH feverishly upheld the cause of human rights. It was instrumental in getting the release of 35 political prisoners, held since 1977 for so-called "crimes of opinion." By linking its objectives to world standards and intelligently subsuming Islamic tradition under those standards, the OMDH openly identified itself with the international cause for human rights. The French newspaper, *Le Monde*, published at least 17 articles directly relating to the OMDH. Originally, the OMDH called for abrogation of legislation that diminished the practice of liberty. It also planned for the collection of legal documents to establish relations with international human rights organizations. Pressurized by the OMDH, King Hassan II was obliged to create the Human Rights Consultative Council in Morocco.

Reference: Susan Waltz, "Making Waves: The Political Impact of Human Rights Groups in North Africa," *Journal of Modern African Studies* 29 (3), 1991: 481-504.

MOSAIKO CULTURAL CENTER. (Angola).

Some church groups have shown interest in involving themselves effectively in defending human rights in Angola. One such initiative is that of the Dominican order, which has been trying to raise funds to complete its Mosaiko Cultural

Center outside Luanda. One activity proposed for this center is the promotion of justice and human rights. It hopes to act as a resource center for reports on human rights in war torn Angola, and to provide a forum for discussions of human rights. The cultural center translated human rights articles of consequences into Portuguese and other languages. The center also has been engaged in an outreach mission to educate people around the country about their civic rights.

Reference: Human Rights Watch, *Angola* (New York: Human Rights Watch, 1996).

MOVEMENT FOR FREEDOM AND JUSTICE (MFJ). (Ghana).

Since 1981, Jerry Rawling's military government used the paramilitary to abuse people's civil rights and the government's Civil Defense Organization (CDO) used excessive force to suppress civil rights upholders. The MFJ operated against these abuses. This nonpolitical organization, founded in 1990, campaigned for democracy, democratic principles in government, and general human rights in Ghana. In August 1990, the organization claimed that one of its executive members, Daniel Kaba, was killed by two CDO members. In October 1990, nine members of the MFJ were arrested by the military government.

Reference: Human Rights Internet, *Occasional Papers October 1992 (Ghana)* (Boston, MA: Harvard Law School, 1989).

MOVEMENT FOR PEACE IN MOZAMBIQUE. (Mozambique).

The Rome Accord ended the brutal 19-year civil war in the country, although violations of the cease-fire continued to occur in 1993. According to the Rome Accord, multiparty elections were to be held in 1994. Several nongovernmental human rights organizations were established with defined constituencies and goals. The Movement for Peace in Mozambique was set up in 1993. It aimed to involve all sectors of Mozambican society to safeguard the peace process and maintain political peace so that opposing groups would honor human rights.

Reference: US Department of State, *Country Reports on Human Rights Practices for 1993* (Washington, D.C.: Government Printing Office, 1994).

MOVEMENT FOR THE DEFENCE OF HUMAN RIGHTS AND LIBERTIES (MDDHL). (Cameroon).

This group reports on arbitrary arrest and ill treatment of political detainees. It is based in Maroua in the Far North Province in Cameroon.

Reference: Amnesty International, USA, *Amnesty International Report, 1996* (New York: Amnesty International, 1996).

MOVEMENT FOR THE SURVIVAL OF THE OGONI PEOPLE (MOSOP). (Nigeria).

The Port Harcourt-based human rights group is critical of the partnership between the government and the foreign oil companies. It questioned the role of the Shell company whose role appeared to be illegitimate to the people in Ogoniland. The Ogoni are a distinct ethnic minority of about 500,000 people, who occupy the northeastern fringes of the Niger Delta in southeastern Nigeria. The Movement alleged that the River State governor promulgated laws to detain protesters belonging to the minority. It argued that a critical human rights issue in Nigeria in the early 1990s was the severe repression of the Ogoni ethnic group in the oil-producing Niger Delta region.

Its demands are now several. First, it demands protection against governmental atrocities. It alleges that military regimes have systematically violated Ogoni people's political rights. As the part of the **Campaign for Democracy,** this organization is devoted to the restoration of democracy and asks for more political rights. The new struggle of the MOSOP has been for the restoration of the multiparty democracy in Nigeria. This approach has provided a new opportunity for articulating issues that directly affected the nonbourgeois: children, women, rural people, the unemployed, and popular communities.

Second, its strategy is empowerment of victimized ethnic groups. In 1993, the Ogoni protested in marches against various exploitations by the Federal Government and the Shell Petroleum Development Company (Nigeria) Limited. The MOSOP claimed that about 1,000 people, including women and children, had been killed between July and October 1993. Many villages were also destroyed. The movement skillfully drew international attention through publications, lobbying (especially within the UN), and high-profile leadership. After an unsuccessful one-year wait for an audience with President Ibrahim Babangida, the MOSOP made representation to "all international bodies which have a role to play in the preservation of our nationality." The MOSOP's message was made clear: the Ogoni people in the Delta state should get not only more revenues from oil but also more political rights. In 1993, its president Ken Saro-Wiwa, a well-known Nigerian writer, took steps to highlight rights issues. His book, *Genocide in Nigeria: The Ogoni Tragedy*, was written in a mode of frustration. No Nigerian in recent years has wielded a pen more effectively than Saro-Wiwa to defend people's rights. He was arrested by the Nigerian government in 1993 and 1994. The African Commission tried to plead on behalf of Saro-Wiwa. In November 1995, Saro-Wiwa and eight others were executed.

Third, oil drilling had been responsible for the destruction of the environment in Ogoniland, and this destruction led to protests by the Ogonis. The movement claims that land, streams, and creeks have already been polluted by foreign oil companies. When the MOSOP loudly protested, the federal government, in retaliation, led a campaign of brutal persecution. On behalf of oil companies (Shell-BP), the army, led by generals, intervened to suppress protests there. These repressive tactics have forced the movement to widen the scope of human rights demands. It now asks for the protection of the Ogoni environment and ecology from further degradation as well as more autonomy for the people in the state. Recently; Shell announced that it would explicitly acknowledge respect for human rights and the environment in its revamped internal code of conduct.

References: Human Rights Watch, "Human Rights in Africa and US Policy" New York: Human Rights Watch, 1994; Claude E. Welch, Jr., *Protecting Human Rights in Africa: Roles and Strategies of Non-Governmental Organizations* (Philadelphia: University of Pennsylvania, 1995); Ken Saro-Wiwa, *Genocide in Nigeria: The Ogoni Tragedy* (London: Saros, 1992).

MOVEMENT OF DEMOCRATIC CASAMANCE FORCES (MFDC). (Senegal).
Casamance, a less developed area of Senegal, has been

physically isolated. It is inhabited primarily by Diola which
have pressed for greater autonomy. Feelings of neglect and
suppression by the central government have supported the
MFDC's ethnic appeal. The Senegalese government has
vigorously countered its separatism. The Casamance issue
remains one of Senegal's most persistent human rights
problems. The MFDC argues that the people's political rights
have been abridged.

Reference: Claude E. Welch, Jr. *Protecting Human Rights in Africa*
(Philadelphia: University of Pennsylvania Press, 1995).

MOZAMBICAN CAMPAIGN TO BAN LANDMINES (CMCM).
(Mozambique).

The CMCM was formally launched in November 1995. Since
1992, landmines in Mozambique have claimed some 10,000
victims. The CMCM obtained a high media profile during the
1997 Maputo-held Fourth International NGO Conference to
Ban Landmines. It presented to President Chissano its petition
of over 100,000 signatures in support of a total ban. It was
also active during the Oslo conference on the banning of
landmines. This NGO helped organize the fourth conference
of the International Campaign to Ban Landmines held in
Maputo in Mozambique from February 25-28, 1997.

References: Human Rights Watch, *World Report 1998* (New York:
Human Rights Watch, 1998); Human Rights Watch, *Still Killing:
Landmines in Southern Africa* (New York: Human Rights Watch, 1997).

MOZAMBICAN HUMAN RIGHTS ASSOCIATION.
(Mozambique).

This new organization is different from the **Mozambican
League of Human Rights**. It was formed in May 1996 with a
primary mission of providing human rights education as well
as educating the public about general human rights.

Reference: US Department of State, *Country Reports on Human Rights
Practices for 1993* (Washington, D.C.: Government Printing Office,
1994).

MOZAMBICAN LEAGUE OF HUMAN RIGHTS. (Liga
Mocambicana dos Direitos do Hommen) (LDH). (Mozambique).

There were no legal obstacles to the formation of human rights
groups in Mozambique. The LDH was primarily organized by

Maria Alice Mabota, a law student in the Faculty of Law of the Eduardo Mondlane University (UEM), who was in contact with other Portuguese-speaking countries in Africa. Following the blue prints of the constitution of the **Human Rights League of Guinea-Bissau**, Mabota drew up a constitution and held meetings in several cities. Gradually, intellectuals, members of the press, and university faculties joined the organization. It became more active in late 1993, held a public meeting in Maputo, and developed plans for human rights education as well as monitoring programs relating to various rights. However, the primary goals, strategies, and methods of the LDH have not yet been clearly defined. Areas of immediate concern are the state prisons, abuses by public officials, in particular the police, and the increasing poverty of the people. The LDH held a conference in 1997 in Maputo on the role of parliamentarians in the promotion and defense of human rights.

References: US Department of State, *Country Reports on Human Rights Practices for 1993* (Washington, D.C.: Government Printing Office, 1994); University of Minnesota Human Rights Library, "Human Rights," http://www.umn.edu/humanrts/africa/mozambiq.htm

MOZAMBIQUE WOMEN'S ORGANIZATION (OMM).
(Mozambique).

This association is engaged in raising the legal and economic status of women in community villages in Mozambique. The OMM insists that the age of prospective spouses be publicized and that the authorities grant approval for marriage only when those to be married are old enough. Polygamous marriages are strongly discouraged by the group. But most rural Mozambicans do not live in communal villages, and as such it is difficult to know whether traditional social practices have really been abolished.

Reference: Harold D. Nelson (ed.), *Mozambique: A Country Study* (Washington, D.C.: Government Printing Office, 1984).

N

NADIM CENTER FOR THE MANAGEMENT AND REHABILITATION OF VICTIMS OF VIOLENCE. (Egypt).

This Cairo-based NGO maintained that torture by police was a nationwide phenomenon, and it exposed various methods of torture that had been used on its clients including: beating with sticks and whips, kicking with boots, electric shocks, and suspension from one or both arms. The Nadim noted that in all cases victims had been threatened. The group issues reports and findings.

Reference: Human Rights Watch, *World Report 1998* (New York: Human Rights Watch, 1998).

NAMIBIAN WOMEN'S ORGANIZATION. (Namibia).

Violence against women, including beating and rape, has been widespread in Namibia. This group has asked for drastic measures against rapists. It was satisfied when the High Court punished a convicted rapist to life imprisonment. The Namibian Women's Organization has asked the government to be stricter in dealing with crimes against women.

Reference: US Department of State, *Country Reports for Human Rights Practices for 1996* (Washington, D.C.: Government Printing Office, 1997).

NATIONAL ASSOCIATION OF DEMOCRATIC LAWYERS (NAODL). (South Africa).

This private association has set up legal services in rural areas in South Africa. Under its umbrella, a new paralegal training project was set up in the Eastern Cape Province, a region that used to be, before 1994, hard-hit by political repression. The association focused on "services and resources on human rights violations, particularly in rural areas."

Reference: International Commission of Jurists, *Paralegals in Rural Areas* (Geneva, Switzerland: International Commission of Jurists, 1991).

NATIONAL ASSOCIATION OF DEMOCRATIC LAWYERS IN NIGERIA (NAODLIN). (Nigeria).

An unintended result of the Babangida regime's random violations of civil and political rights was the emergence of the NAODLIN, an advocacy group of legal practitioners. The group challenged the Nigerian government's detention of civilians and also led campaigns to stop the election of General Olusegun Obasanjo as the UN Secretary General. It argued that when Obasanjo served as Nigeria's head of state, his government was responsible for numerous human rights abuses. One of its strategies was organizing a series of campaigns to prevent Bola Ajibola from being appointed to the World Court at the Hague. This group used its tactics in a sophisticated way so as to avoid direct confrontation with the government.

Reference: Eileen McCarthy-Arnolds et al., *Africa, Human Rights, and the Global System* (Westport, CT: Greenwood Press, 1994).

NATIONAL ASSOCIATION OF NGOs (NANGO). (Zimbabwe).

This private national group is free to act so long as its activities are not political. It opposes the government's Private Voluntary Organizations Act of 1995, which could suspend the work of private organizations. To avoid any conflict with the government, the organization calls itself an association so that there would be less interference from the government.

Reference: US Department of State, *Country Reports for Human Rights Practices for 1993*. (Washington, D.C.: Government Printing Office, 1994).

NATIONAL ASSOCIATION OF NIGERIAN STUDENTS (NANS). (Nigeria).

In the 1990s, this nongovernmental association became critical of the human rights abuses of the government of Nigeria. In 1992, its President, Olusegun Mayegun, was arrested and jailed. This student body has a program calling for respect for human rights.

Reference: Brendalyn P. Ambrose, *Democratization and the Protection of Human Rights in Africa* (Westport, CT: Praeger, 1995).

NATIONAL ASSOCIATION OF SEA DOGS (NASD). (Nigeria). This NGO fought against the Structural Adjustment Program (SAP) through civil unrest. Physical intimidation and imprisonment of protest leaders were the harsh responses by the Babangida government. As an alternative to SAP, the NASD suggested other means for economic and social reforms. It held meetings and conferences for publicity. The government prevented the NASD from holding conferences and therefore the government's action was interpreted by the group as a breach of rights.

Reference: Eileen McCarthy-Arnolds et al., *Africa, Human Rights, and the Global System* (Westport, CT: Greenwood press, 1994).

NATIONAL CHILDREN IN NEED NETWORK (NCNN). (Kenya). In 1995, this group complained that the Kenyan penal code did not pay any respect to street children, who received punishment as criminals. It argued that preliminary efforts to modify laws were good, but not enough to lend protection to street children. It demanded substantive changes in laws relating to the punishment of children.

Reference: Human Rights Watch, *Juvenile Injustice* (New York: Human Rights Watch, 1997).

NATIONAL CHILDREN'S RIGHTS COMMITTEE. (South Africa). This Braamfontein-based center considers child abuse a human rights issue. Through education, it argues that there are rights such as the child's right to survive, the right to develop, and the right to be protected. The center is against pornography involving children, and it opposes child labor.

Reference: International Commission of Jurists, *Schools for Peace* (Geneva, Switzerland: EIP, 1996).

NATIONAL COMMISSION OF HUMAN RIGHTS (CNDH).
(Togo).

The CNDH was created by law in Lome in 1987 with the help of judges and lawyers, and it was charged with providing an internal mechanism for assuring the protection of human rights. In 1988, it organized a national seminar on human rights to discuss how to stop casesy of torture and also how socio-economic rights could be achieved. In 1993, it complained that its former chairman, Dr. Robert A. Dovi, was forced to take refuge in Benin after receiving threats from soldiers.

References: Human Rights Internet, *Human Rights Internet: Reporter* (Boston, MA: Harvard Law School, February 1994); Amnesty International USA, *Report* (New York: Hunter House Publishers, 1996).

NATIONAL COMMISSION ON HUMAN RIGHTS. (Chad).

This group was established in 1994. Composed of both governmental and nongovernmental representatives, it urged the Chadian government to redefine the role of the ANS (National Security Agency), which had a record of serious human rights violations. It works through appeal to the government.

Reference: Amnesty International USA, *Amnesty International Report 1996* (New York: Amnesty International Publications, 1996).

NATIONAL COMMITTEE FOR THE STRUGGLE AGAINST THE VESTIGES OF SLAVERY IN MAURITANIA. (Mauritania).

This nongovernmental group focuses on overcoming the vestiges of slavery. Mauritanians continue to suffer from the effects of the generations of practice of slavery in Moor society, and of caste distinctions that include slaves in Afro-Mauritanian societies. There are still paid and unpaid slaves. In fact, many consider themselves as slaves. Punishment is rare for individuals who break the state law prohibiting slavery in any form. The National Committee for the Struggle Against the Vestiges of Slavery in Mauritania addresses the human rights issues pertaining to slavery to raise public awareness.

Reference: US Department of State, *Country Reports for Human Rights Practices for 1993* (Washington, D.C.: Government Printing Office, 1994).

NATIONAL CONVENTION EXECUTIVE COUNCIL (NCEC). (Kenya).

A wide variety of human rights monitoring groups are engaged in reporting rights violations in Kenya. In particular, the NCEC, a prodemocracy alliance made up of a coalition of religious leaders, human rights workers and political activists began to operate effectively. It came under governmental attack in 1997. The government criticized the council because it had asked for democratic reforms.

Reference: Human Rights Watch, *World Report 1998* (New York: Human Rights Watch, 1998).

NATIONAL COUNCIL FOR CHILDREN. (Seychelles).

There are no private groups devoted exclusively to investigating human rights practices in Seychelles, and very few child-abuse cases are actually prosecuted in court. The strongest public advocate for young victims is this semi-autonomous agency, the National Council for Children, which claims that the police do not investigate child-abuse cases with enough vigor.

Reference: US Department of State, *Country Reports for Human Rights Practices for 1993* (Washington, D.C.: Government Printing Office, 1994).

NATIONAL COUNCIL OF KENYA CHURCHES (NCCK). (Kenya).

To the annoyance of President Moi, the NCCK remained a strong agency capable of openly challenging human rights abuses in Kenya. Harassment of the clergy intensified in 1989. The NCCK spoke strongly on the queuing system, a system by which a parliamentary candidate was required to ask voters to line up behind the photograph of the candidate of their choice. Members of the NCCK argued that the government had "demanded that disciplinary measures be taken against these clergy men because of the manner in which they exercise their freedoms of speech and of worship. Recently clergymen have been interrogated by the police about contents of sermons they had given in church." According to the group, it was an infringement of freedom of conscience.

Reference: Africa Watch, A Committee on Human Rights Watch, *Kenya* (Washington, D.C.: Human Rights Watch, 1990).

NATIONAL COUNCIL OF WOMEN OF KENYA (NCWK).
(Kenya).

As one of the most important nongovernmental women's organizations, established in 1964, this group was engaged in rights issues. The NCWK, like the **Maendeleo Ya Wanawake Organization (MYWO)**, developed into a nationally based organization with the primary objective of coordinating other women's organizations and groups in Kenya. After 1975, under the leadership of its controversial chairman, Professor Wangari Mathai, it became instrumental in initiating and developing the Green-Belt tree planting movement. Unlike the MYWO, the NCWK's role seems to have gradually diminished, as the Women's Decade came to a close. As an NGO, the NCWK has attempted to take a position on national issues and make demands for legislative changes on issues where women's rights are adversely affected.

Reference: Maria Nzomo, "The Impact of the Women's Decade on Policies, Programs and Empowerment of Women in Kenya," *Issue* (Summer, 1989): 9-17.

NATIONAL DEMOCRATIC AND HUMAN RIGHTS ORGANIZATION (NDEHURIO). (Kenya).

Kenya reintroduced multiparty democracy in 1991, but President Moi and his KANU party tolerated no opposition voice in Kenya. The year 1992 witnessed serious setbacks in the government's commitment to human rights. The government intimidated its critics. The NDEHURIO was established as a human rights group by Koigi Wa Wamwere in 1993 to focus on the issue of ethnic clashes caused by partisan politicians in Kenya. The government arrested its members. In September 1993, seven members of the group were brought to court in Nakuru where they complained that they were beaten by the police. Charges were brought against Wambere and Kariuki for "administering an unlawful oath." The NDEHURIO was denied registration. Koigi Wa Wamwere, a political activist and a nemesis to President Moi and his KANU party, remained a leading figure of the NDEHURIO, which, at the instance of these prominent leaders, has conducted investigations into the government-sponsored tribal clashes in the Rift Valley.

References: Africa Watch, *Divide and Rule (Kenya)* (New York:

Human Rights Watch, 1993); Keith B. Richburg, *Out of America* (New York: Basic Books, 1997).

NATIONAL ENVIRONMENTAL ACCESSIBILITY PROGRAM.
(South Africa).

In practice, both the government and the private sector's discrimination in employment still exists in South Africa. Recently this NGO, comprising disabled consumers as well as service providers, has established a presence in all nine provinces to lobby for compliance with the government regulations for hiring disabled persons and to sue offending property owners when necessary. This society offers a modern concept of people with disabilities as a minority whose civil rights must be protected.

Reference: US Department of State, *Country Reports for Human Rights Practices for 1993* (Washington, D.C.: Government Printing Office, 1997).

NATIONAL HUMAN RIGHTS CENTER OF LIBERIA. (Liberia).

This coalition group to monitor rights violations functioned relatively freely in Monrovia in 1997. The proposed governmental Commission for Human Rights was supposed to take members from this group as well.

Reference: Human Rights Watch, *World Report 1998* (New York: Human Rights Watch, 1998).

NATIONAL INSTITUTE FOR CRIME PREVENTION AND THE REHABILITATION OF OFFENDERS (NICRO). (South Africa).

This group, based in Cape Town, has tried to make arrangements with the government to be able to visit prisoners and provide legal assistance. This contact group provides free legal assistance to victims. It also pleads for children's rights.

Reference: Africa Watch, *Prison Conditions in South Africa* (New York: Human Rights Watch, 1994).

NATIONAL LEAGUE FOR DEFENSE OF HUMAN RIGHTS.
(Niger).

Since the peace pact between the government and the separatists in 1995, the government usually tolerated investigations by human rights groups, although a certain kind of intimidation has prevailed. The National League highlights

abuses committed both by the government and the separatists.
Reference: US Department of State, *Country Reports for Human Rights Practices for 1993* (Washington, D.C.: Government Printing Office, 1997).

NATIONAL LEAGUE FOR FREE AND FAIR ELECTIONS (LINELIT). (Democratic Republic of Congo, formerly Zaire).

This local NGO reports on torture and inhumane treatment at the hands of the police in Zaire. It claimed that two members of the **Union for Democracy and Social Progress** in 1993 were arrested and tortured by the security forces because of the dissidents' political beliefs. The government rarely responds to human rights accusations but it permits the LINELIT to operate with some restrictions.

Reference: US Department of State, *Country Reports for Human Rights Practices for 1993* (Washington, D.C.: Government Printing Office, 1997).

NATIONAL LEAGUE FOR HUMAN RIGHTS (NLHR). (Burkina Faso).

The NLHR was established in August 1987 to publicize cases of human rights abuses. It sought both collective and individual democratic rights as well as the right to freedom of speech for all citizens.

Reference: Human Rights Internet, *Human Rights Internet: Reporter* (Boston, MA: Harvard Law School, February 1994).

NATIONAL LEAGUE FOR HUMAN RIGHTS (NLHR). (Cameroon).

Although multiparty elections were held in 1992, the flawed presidential race represented a step backward in Cameroon's democratization process. Members of the President's ethnic group, the Beti, wield a disproportionate share of political power, particularly in key economic and security portfolios. Although domestic and international human rights monitoring groups were permitted to operate in Cameroon, their effectiveness was impeded by governmental interference. Nongovernmental organizations, such as the NLHR and others, were and are still engaged in the collection of data with respect to various aspects of rights violations. Financial hardships, inexperience, and fear of reprisals have so far discouraged these civic associations from publicly criticizing the government's human rights record. Therefore, the NLHR sought primarily to heighten awareness of human rights issues rather than investigate specific alleged violations. To accomplish these objectives, they distributed informational publications and held awareness clinics and meetings in towns and rural centers. It may be noted that the presidentially appointed National Commission for Human Rights and Freedom failed to report publicly its findings of investigations into allegations of human rights abuses.

Reference: US Department of State, *Country Reports for Human Rights Practices for 1993* (Washington, D.C.: Government Printing Office, 1994).

NATIONAL MONITORING BODY FOR HUMAN RIGHTS (ONDH). (Algeria).

The ONDH is a semi-official organization, engaged, among other things, in recording human casualties caused by armed Islamists who are opposed to the government. Violent acts by armed Islamist groups increased dramatically in Algeria during 1993, as did the efforts of the Algerian government security forces to crush the resistance. About 100 Islamists were killed by the security forces in November 1993, eiher Islamists or civilians. The ONDH records killings of persons in custody as well as the targeted assassination of civilians, whether by government forces or by armed opposition groups. This organization believes that human rights abuses by one party, no matter how egregious, never justifies violations committed by another party.

Reference: Middle East Watch, *Human Rights Abuses in Algeria: No One is Spared* (New York: Human Rights Watch, 1994).

NATIONAL ORGANIZATION FOR CIVIC EDUCATION AND ELECTIONS MONITORING. (Uganda).

This organization deals with concerns related to civil society and political rights in Uganda after each new government comes to power. One of its main tasks is to report on general elections.

Reference: US Department of State, *Country Reports for Human Rights Practices for 1993* (Washington, D.C.: Government Printing Office, 1997).

NATIONAL ORGANIZATION OF ALGERIAN LAWYERS (ONAA). (Algeria).

This group of defense lawyers acts as a protest organization against the military government's Legislative Decree of 1992. Protests by these lawyers became more vocal over the conduct of Special Court trials that began in March 1993. Lawyers representing the "Emir Noh group," the first group of defendants to be tried before the military special court, withdrew from the trial three times. One objection of the ONAA was that the government added an amendment to the existing regulations, which provided that all defense lawyers would be subject to approval by the Special Court. On May 1993, attorneys in the eastern city of Annaba announced a boycott of the Special Court. Lawyers affiliated with the **Algerian League for the Defense of Human Rights** also, on these grounds, refused to plead before the Special Courts. The ONAA claimed that the trial of Allam Abdennour, an Islamist militant leader also known as "Emir Noh," and fifty codefendants, reflected some of the violations of defendants' due-process rights which are endemic in the Special Courts of Algeria.

Reference: Middle East Watch, *Human Rights Abuses in Algeria: No One is Spared* (New York: Human Rights Watch, 1994).

NATIONAL SOCIETY FOR HUMAN RIGHTS (NSHR). (Namibia).

There are some controversies over the SWAPO party's incomplete accounting of missing detainees held in Angola and Zambia during the preindependence period. There are allegations that the current government has restrictive policies on refugees and that there are forced deportations of asylum seekers. In fact, the preindependence policy of racial discrimination and disparities continued up to 1993. In September 1993, a female refugee at the Osire camp formally charged a police officer with assault and torture. The NSHR agreed to press her case in court. She has since left Namibia and the court cannot make any progress without her presence. In 1993, this society was headed by Phi Ya Nangolah. With its limited resources, small office in the capital city of Windhoek, and a fax machine it collects its information about indiscriminate police detention and other abuses. Phi developed serious reservations about SWAPO's commitment to preventing or correcting human rights abuses. The NSHR's documentation was frequently criticized by SWAPO party supporters. However, this organization is tolerated in the government-controlled press.

References: Claude E. Welch, Jr., *Protecting Human Rights in Africa* (Philadelphia: University of Pennsylvania Press, 1995); US Department of State, *Country Reports for Human Rights Practices for 1993* (Washington, D.C.: Government Printing Office, 1994).

NATIONAL UNION OF MAURITANIAN WOMEN. (Mauritania).

This political party-sponsored women's union was created in 1961. At first it was oriented toward typically feminine issues, such as health, nutrition, and education. By 1964, it had become the women's political base and was renamed the **National Women's Movement (Mouvement National Feminin).** Gradually, it called for the obligatory registration of marriages and divorces to protect women's social status. It also asked for the enactment of laws to discourage polygyny and dowries. The Union's advocacy was partly successful when President Taya named a few women to cabinet level posts.

Reference: Robert E. Handloff, ed., *Mauritania: A Country Study* (Washington, D.C.: Department of State, 1990).

NATIONAL WOMEN'S COALITION. (South Africa).

In South Africa, battered women's own relatives often discourage them from reporting assault because of the shame that disclosure may bring to the entire family. Many women do not want to report cases of rape and other abuses. The National Women's Coalition reported that women's reluctance to report abuses to the police and government legal and social services stemmed directly from their negative experiences with the police. One goal of this association is to collect data of battered women to create awareness.

Reference: The Human Rights Watch, *Global Report on Women's Human Rights* (New York: Human Rights Watch, 1995).

NETWORK FOR HUMAN RIGHTS IN LIBERIA (NFHRIL). (USA).

In Liberia, there are many right groups organized by citizens. This small group is based in the United States, in Virginia.

This private network for human rights in civil-war affected Liberia has been working as a nonpolitical rights group. It is engaged in publicizing rights violations and works closely with some Liberians in the United States and some international organizations.

Reference: Human Rights Internet, Harvard Law School, *Human Rights Internet: Reporter* (Boston, MA: Harvard Law School, February 1994).

NETWORK FOR THE INTEGRATION AND DIFFUSION OF RIGHTS IN THE RURAL MILIEU. (RIDD-FITILA). (Niger).

This group issues declarations and reports to raise public awareness about human rights among the rural population in Niger. After the introduction of the new constitution in 1992, the government conducted multiparty elections for president and national assembly. But the government had to deal with the Tuareg insurgency. Tuareg detainees were held by the government and hostages were held by the rebels. The ethnic minorities such as Tuareg, Fulani, Toubou, and Arabs claimed that the far more numerous Hausa and Djerma ethnic groups discriminated against the minorities. The network reports these discriminations.

Reference: US Department of State, *Country Reports for Human Rights Practices for 1993* (Washington, D.C.: Government Printing Office, 1994).

NETWORK OF AFRICAN RESEARCHERS AND INTELLECTUALS ON INTEGRATED HUMAN RIGHTS IN AFRICA (NARIHRA). (Mozambique).

In 1991, lawyers from throughout Africa met in Mozambique to discuss human rights issues in the continent. A year later, another workshop helped create the NARIHRA under the presidency of Teodosio Uta. Shadrack Gutto, a Kenyan lawyer, became the Secretary General of the organization. Its Executive Committee had members from Senegal, Ethiopia, and Egypt. In the first year of its operation, it had office space and a post box number. The organization can not yet register in Mozambique.

Reference: University of Minnesota Human Rights Library, "Human Rights," http://www.umn.edu/humanrts/africa/mozambiq.htm

NEW NIGERIAN YOUTH MOVEMENT (NNYM). (Nigeria).

This Bamako, Mali, based political organization of exiled Nigerian youths has called for freedom, democracy, and fundamental human rights in Nigeria. Its main aim is to sensitize the Nigerians to the acts of political repression and torture being perpetuated by the present military junta on helpless Nigerians. This private association, operating since October 1996, is open to union leaders, journalists, and human rights campaigners. It has a written constitution.

Reference: New Nigerian Youth Movement, http://www.uib.no/isf /people/campaign/nnnym.htm (May 18,1998).

NIGERIAN BAR ASSOCIATION (NBA). (Nigeria).

In 1979, the NBA established the Human Rights Committee to monitor any misuse of ministerial and administrative powers by the Nigerian government. This was significant because Nigeria had established a civilian rule in 1979 after more than a decade of military rule. The Committee was asked to monitor the government's infringements on the independence of the judges. Human Rights Committees in several states in Nigeria provide legal assistance to victims of human rights abuse and work to protect the rights of prisoners and detainees. The NBA's journal, *Law and Practice*, provides grim details in instances of death of subjects and detainees in police custody. Several reports carried statements from victims of police brutality as well as findings of in-depth investigations by the **Civil Liberties Organization**, which is based in Lagos. In 1984, the NBA complained that by promulgating decrees with "ouster clauses," the Babangida regime was able to use the judicial system as an instrument of repression while it freed itself from accountability. A former president of the NBA, Alao Aka-Bashorun, argued that the political repression under the Babangida administration was systematically done through the enactment of "decrees" having retroactive effect. The NBA is quite active in recording and reporting human rights abuses, committed by the government.

References: M.A. Ajomo and Isabella Okagbue (eds.), *Human Rights and the Administration of Criminal Justice in Nigeria* (Nigerian Institute of Advanced Studies, 1991); Etim Anim, "Confronting Decree 2," *Newswatch* 13 (August 21, 1989).

NIGERIAN INSTITUTE OF ADVANCED LEGAL STUDIES (NIALS). (Nigeria).

In conjunction with the Department of Jurisprudence and International Law, the NIALS held a conference on human rights education in rural environments. Topics included the concept of peoples' rights in the African Charter, the right of legal aid services, and the rights of women in the rural sector. The NIALS complained that prisoners were one of the most afflicted but least prominent groups in Africa. The NIALS further revealed distressing facts about prisoners in Nigeria. Its study in June 1989 revealed that about 58,000 prisoners were being housed in prisons meant for 28,000 inmates, under unhealthy conditions. According to its reports, in the wake of Nigeria's slide into anarchy in the late 1980s and early 1990s, basic human rights were more directly affected by harsh police activities than by those of any other agencies. According to its analysis, only 8 percent of those arrested knew of their right to remain silent; 35.9 percent were slapped. The NIALS's reports provided important data that not only confirmed popular awareness but also challenged were slapped. It's reports provided important data that confirmed popular awareness and also challenged the government to respond. But the Babangida regime did not act favorably.

References: Claude E. Welch, *Protecting Human Rights in Africa* (Philadelphia: University of Pennsylvania, 1995); A. Ajomo and B. Okabue, *Human Rights and the Administration of Criminal Justice in Nigeria* (Lagos, Nigeria: privately published, 1992); Human Rights Internet, *Reporter* (Boston, MA: Harvard Law School, 1989).

NIGERIEN ASSOCIATION FOR THE DEFENSE OF HUMAN RIGHTS (ANDDH). (Niger).

This independent association operates without governmental hindrance. It acts mainly through public declarations, private discourse, articles, and appeals in the press to raise public awareness about rights in rural areas.

Reference: US Department of State, *Country Reports for Human Rights Practices for 1993* (Washington, D.C.: Government Printing Office, 1994).

NISAA INSTITUTE FOR WOMEN'S DEVELOPMENT. (South Africa).

This NGO operates shelters for women in need, and it conducts occasional training sessions on violence against women, for police and judicial officers. This group asks for systematic reforms in women's matters.

Reference: Human Rights Watch, *Violence Against Women in South Africa* (New York: Africa Watch, 1995).

NONGOVERNMENTAL ORGANIZATION COORDINATION COMMITTEE (NGOCC). (Zambia).

The **NGOCC** operates without any governmental interference in Zambia. In collaboration with Young Women Christian Association (Zambia), it promotes women's special rights as well as civil rights.

Reference: US Department of State, *Country Reports for Human Rights Practices for 1993* (Washington, D.C.: Government Printing Office; 1994).

NON-VIOLENCE EVANGELIQUE. (Democratic Republic of Congo, formerly Zaire).

Since 1990, human rights and prodemocracy organizations and other civic groups have been able to function for civic rights. This group arose from local churches. It supported protests in 1992 for democracy and free elections. This organization has been able to investigate governmental and electoral abuses and to publish reports critical of the government.

Reference: Human Rights Watch, *Zaire* (New York: Human Rights Watch, 1997).

NYAE NYAE DEVELOPMENT FOUNDATION (NNDF). (Namibia).

This group works for ethnic rights. As a local NGO, it is engaged in ensuring that primary school materials take San cultural sensibilities into account. The San people, the earliest inhabitants, have been traditionally exploited by other ethnic groups. The NNDF receives cooperation from the Ministry of Education and Culture.

Reference: US Department of State, *Country Reports for Human Rights Practices for 1993* (Washington, D.C.: Government Printing Office, 1994).

O

OBSERVATOIRE NATIONAL DES ELECTIONS (ONE). (Ivory Coast).

This umbrella group of local NGOs received official recognition and government cooperation for observing elections and monitoring the status of civil rights.

Reference: US Department of State, *Country Reports on Human Rights Practices for 1996* (Washington, D.C.: Government Printing Office, 1997).

OGADEN HUMAN RIGHTS COMMITTEE. (Ethiopia).

The Ethiopian government is reluctant to provide legal status to human rights monitoring groups. The Ogaden Human Rights Committee was organized in 1995 to operate clandestinely after the closure of its office in Gode in Somali Region. In June 1996, the police raided the office of the Ogaden committee. Thereafter the group published its reports outside the country.

Reference: Human Rights Watch, *World Report 1998* (New York: Human Rights Watch, 1998).

ORDER OF ETHIOPIA (OE). (South Africa).

The OE was founded by a black Anglican minister in the early 1990s. It incorporated elements of black religious culture in South Africa. In the 1980s, it became engaged in upholding human rights of blacks. As it took part in peace talks with the government, it suffered police harassment.

Reference: Human Rights Watch, *No Neutral Ground: South Africa's Confrontation with Activist Churches* (New York: US Department of State, 1989).

ORDER OF LAWYERS OF MOZAMBIQUE (OLM).
(Mozambique).

The OLM lobbied for higher standards for the legal profession. It is a human rights monitor group.

Reference: Human Rights Watch, *World Report* (New York: Human Rights Watch, 1998).

ORGANIZATION CONGOLAISE DES DROITS DE L'HOMME (OCDH). (Republic of Congo).

Civilians in the Republic of Congo, now under a democratically elected president after 24 years of one-party rule, continue to employ vigilante justice against presumed thieves and sorcerers who are sometimes beaten to death. Congo's leading human rights watch group, the OCDH, reported 11 such killings. The organization laments that no judicial actions followed. Its focus is vigilante justice.

Reference: US Department of State, *Country Reports on Human Rights Practices for 1996* (Washington, D.C.: Government Printing Office, 1997).

ORGANIZATION FOR HUMAN RIGHTS AND FREEDOMS.
(Cameroon).

This organization is engaged in the collection of data regarding rights abuses. It has limited resources, and it has not been very effective.

Reference: US Department of State, *Country Reports on Human Rights Practices for 1996* (Washington, D.C.: Government Printing Office, 1997).

ORGANIZATION OF AFRICAN UNITY (OAU). (Ethiopia).

Since its inception in 1963, the OAU seemed to function as a club of presidents engaged in a tacit policy of not inquiring into each other's human rights practices. This Addis Ababa-based all African organization has been historically less concerned with human rights, and more concerned with self-determination, the ending of foreign rule in parts of Africa as well as white settlers' rule in South Africa and South Rhodesia. To attain a measure of moral authority not only outside the continent but even among its own members, the OAU planned to work on human rights issues. The UN also put pressure on the OAU. Thus it agreed in 1981 to endorse the African Charter on Human and Peoples' Rights, which came into existence in October 1986 (**Banjul Charter**). Ineffectual even in its wording, let alone in its implementation, the Charter so far has made very little impact on the rights issues. The prime OAU instrument for ensuring the observance of the various rights is the African Commission on Human and Peoples' Rights. The Commission's eleven members, elected for six -year terms, faced severe limitations because they had been dependent on the African governments, and the governments hardly agreed on rights issues. The Commission, with its headquarters in Banjul, The Gambia, so far failed to do much in human rights partly because of the lack of awareness on the part of individual citizens and also because of the reluctance of individual governments.

References: Claude E. Welch, Jr., "The Organisation of African Unity and the Promotion of Human Rights," *The Journal of Modern African Studies*, vol. 29 (1991); Christopher Clapman, *Africa and the International System* (Cambridge: Cambridge University Press, 1996).

ORGANIZATION OF ANGOLAN WOMEN (OMA). (Angola).

This organization was associated with the main political party, the Popular Movement for the Liberation of Angola. Gradually, it began to operate with relative autonomy. In 1985, its membership rose to 1.8 million. During the 1980s, the OMA set up literary programs and educational opportunities for women. Through the agency of the OMA, some women were employed in health and social services organizations serving refugees and rural families. Its focus has been empowerment of women.

Reference: Thomas Collelo (ed.), *Angola: A Country Study* (Washington, D.C.: Government Printing Office, 1991).

ORGANIZATION OF MOZAMBICAN WOMEN (OMM). (Mozambique).

The OMM attempts to incorporate women into society as a

whole. Through debates and discussions, it brings to reality the powerlessness of women and the power of men. This organization argues that the social structure has devalued the role of women as workers.

Reference: Cindi Corville in *Africa Today* (1st quarter 1990).

OROMO EX-PRISONERS FOR HUMAN RIGHTS. (Ethiopia). The Ethiopian government did not give legal status to human rights organizations. Some Oromo leaders were arrested in 1997 because they spoke against governmental abuses of rights. The Oromo Ex-Prisoners for Human Rights was forced to go into hiding. The group continued to monitor rights violations in the Oromiya regional state and published reports outside Ethiopia.

Reference: Human Rights Watch, *World Report 1998* (New York: Human Rights Watch, 1998).

P

PAN-AFRICAN CENTER FOR RESEARCH ON PEACE, DEVELOPMENT AND HUMAN RIGHTS (PERCEP). (Nigeria).

Based in Nigeria, PERCEP is devoted to research and related intellectual pursuits in the area of linkages between peace, development, and human rights. It has an activist role in seeking policy recommendations arising from research findings and selling such recommendations to the relevant African governments and population. It has largely been interested in the exposition of violations of human rights and as such it organizes seminars and conferences in which usually jurists are invited.

Reference: Issa G. Shivji, *The Concept of Human Rights in Africa* (London: CODESRIA Books, 1989).

PARENTS' COMMITTEE (PC). (Namibia).

The PC was engaged in tracing political detainees in Namibia before independence. In 1989, after the return of the former detainees to the capital of Windhoek, concern about past SWAPO party abuses mounted among the general public in the southern African state of Namibia, formerly known as South West Africa. Several private organizations passed their resolutions on the detainees. The PC, which emerged prominently in the mid-1980s, had at first campaigned quietly for information on the fate of the relatives who went missing in the SWAPO held territory. The group began to openly criticize the abuses of the SWAPO party. In May 1989, the PC brought a court action to secure the release of six people it alleged the SWAPO was holding in detention in Angola. The PC's action coincided with the return of the United Nations Missions on Detainees.

Reference: Human Rights Watch / Africa Watch, *Accounting in Namibia: Human Rights and the Transition to Democracy* (New York: Human Rights Watch, 1992).

PEOPLE OPPOSING WOMEN ABUSE (POWA). (South Africa). This Johannesburg-based nongovernmental rights organization claims that one in six women is abused by her partner and that there are some abusive husbands who will not hesitate to harm their partners if sufficiently angered, despite the possibility of legal penalties. This private group contacts magistrates for interdict to provide relief to the battered women. Because the group addresses domestic violence issues, it has several options. First, it takes into consideration the structural and social factors that place women at risk. Second, it deals with cases of women not only in the city but also outside the city. In 1994, one of its lawyers took up a case from a woman client who claimed that her marriage was threatened by another woman's spouse who wanted to destroy her legal marriage. Third, it publicizes gives publicity of abuses. It reported that, various kinds of abuses of women are quite common. According to a study by the POWA, there were 37,000 rape cases in 1995. The group is seriously concerned with women's marital cases. Last, the group also argues that the greatest obstacle to the effective implementation of the Family Practice Act appears to lie with the police, many of whom are ignorant about the law. A woman, contends the group, possessing a valid interdict may nonetheless receive little protection from law enforcement agents.

References: Human Rights Watch and Africa Watch, *Violence Against Women in South Africa* (New York: Human Rights Watch, 1995); Human Rights Watch, *Global Report on Women's Human Rights* (New York: Human Rights Watch, 1995); US Department of State, *Country Reports on Human Rights Practices for 1996* (Washington, D.C.: Government Printing Office, 1997).

PERMANENT ARAB COMMISSION ON HUMAN RIGHTS.
(Egypt).

There are no authoritative norms regarding human rights issues in the Arab regions bordering Israel and neighboring areas in the Middle East. This group was established in 1968 by the League of Arab States to monitor human rights status. The commission has not been very active, except for occasional efforts to publicize human rights violations in Israeli-occupied territories.

Reference: US Department of State, *Country Reports on Human Rights Practices for 1996* (Washington, D.C.: Government Printing Office, 1997).

POLICE AND PRISON CIVIL RIGHTS UNION (POPCRU). (South Africa).

This unrecognized body began to work for prison reforms in South Africa. Founded in 1989 by a group of "colored" policemen and prison guards, it has been committed to the improvement of working conditions for black and colored prison staff and to the promotion of respect for the civil rights of all prisoners and detainees. In 1993, it was legalized and some unruly members and officers were disciplined by the South African Department of Correctional Services.

Reference: Human Rights Watch, *Prison Conditions in South Africa: Prison Project* (New York: Human Rights Watch, 1994).

POLITICAL CONSULTATIVE COMMITTEE (PCC). (Namibia).

The PCC was formed in Angola as a pressure group by ex-SWAPO detainees shortly before their repatriation to Namibia. Its agenda included efforts to campaign for the release of the detainees still being held and also to publicize the human rights abuses committed by the SWAPO political party. It held several dramatic conferences in Windhoek, where a number of detainees stripped to display the physical scars of their imprisonment. It was declared that much larger numbers were still being held by the SWAPO. After Namibia became independent in March 1990, the detainee question became a focus of this group.

Reference: Human Rights Watch, *Accounting in Namibia* (New York: Human Rights Watch, 1997).

PROGRAM OF ACTION TO MITIGATE THE SOCIAL COSTS OF ADJUSTMENTS (PAMSCAD). (Ghana).

In 1987, the government of Ghana introduced this program to aid needy women and others. It was designed to relieve some of the harsh economic consequences of the Economic Recovery Program and its adjustment dimensions. In 1990, the PAMSCAD stipulated that it would provide credit to women and make facilities for training of women in basic book-keeping and management techniques. In reality, it assisted women in Ghana to acquire simple appropriate technological implements to lighten their workload. Essentially, the PAMSCAD is a framework for the full participation of women in Ghana in accordance with the Convention on the Elimination of All Forms of Discrimination Against Women. Its results are yet to be assessed.

Reference: Rebecca J. Cook (ed.), *Human Rights of Women: National and International Perspectives* (Philadelphia: University of Pennsylvania Press, 1994).

R

RAPE AND INCEST AID. (Mauritius).

According to the Ministry of Women's Rights and Family Welfare, attorneys, and religious and charitable organizations, violence against women is widespread. Police generally are not involved in cases of wife beating. The Rape and Incest Aid has been active in sensitizing the general public about these abuses. This NGO derives some satisfaction because victims are frequently and informally referred to this group by the Mauritian police.

Reference: US Department of State, *Country Reports on Human Rights Practices for 1993* (Washington, D.C.: Government Printing Office, 1994).

RAPE CRISIS. (South Africa).

This Cape Town based group, manned by both men and women, works for the redress of battered women in South Africa. In 1992, Rape Crisis estimated that one in every three women was assaulted by her male partner. The center, realizes that staggering numbers of South African women of all races and income levels face violations, mostly at the hands of men they know and on whom they rely. The crisis center, despite limited resources, has helped women in need.

Reference: *Rape Crisis* (1992), cited in Desiree Hansson and Batie Hofmeyr, *Women's Rights: Towards a Non-Sexist South Africa*, no. 7 (Developing Justice Series) (Witwatersrand, South Africa:

Documentation Center, Center for Legal Studies, University of Witwatersrand, 1992).

REGIONAL COMMITTEE FOR HUMAN RIGHTS DEVELOPMENT (RCHRD). (Eritrea).

Eritrea achieved independence from Ethiopia in 1991, which was under the military rule of General Mengistu. The new government in Eritrea generally respected human rights. One human rights concern as seen by the international organizations has been some kinds of abuses, especially abuses of political detainees. The penalizing code currently in force in Eritrea had been in use during the military rule under Mengistu. "Criminals" are still kept in jail up to 60 days before taken to trial. The RCHRD, an independent group, has exposed the sad prison conditions in Eritrea.

Reference: US Department of State, *Country Reports on Human Rights Practices for 1993* (Washington, D.C.: Government Printing Office, 1994).

RELEASE OF POLITICAL PRISONERS (RPP). (Kenya).

This well-organized pressure group takes account of political detainees in Kenya and produces regular reports on human rights situations. In 1996, it reported that a population of 41,000 prisoners suffered variously in jails. There were torn mattresses, old blankets, and no shoes for prisoners. When the RPP protested these abuses, several of its members were arrested by the government of President Moi in 1996.

Reference: US Department of State, *Country Reports on Human Rights Practices for 1934* (Washington, D.C.: Government Printing Office, 1994).

RWANDAN ASSOCIATION FOR THE DEFENSE OF HUMAN RIGHTS (ARDHO). (Rwanda).

The ARDHO was one of the five Rwandan human rights associations that suffered enormous losses during the genocide in 1996. In February 1997, the founder of Rwanda's first human rights organization — the ARDHO — died suddenly. Authorities failed to investigate allegations that he had been murdered. Emmanuel Hitimana, a researcher with the ARDHO, was detained for seven days and was warned to stop doing human rights work. This activist group reports on

"disappearances" as well.
Reference: Human Rights Watch, *World Reports 1998* (New York: Human Rights Watch, 1998).

RWANDAN ASSOCIATION FOR THE DEFENSE OF HUMAN RIGHTS AND PUBLIC LIBERTIES (ADL). (Rwanda).

This group reports on "disappearances" and extra-judicial killings. Its secretary, Rosalie Mukarukaka, was detained by police in 1997 on suspicion. Under government pressure, this group gave up rigorous monitoring of human rights abuses and remained devoted to less dangerous tasks, like human rights education.
Reference: Human Rights Watch, *World Reports 1998* (New York: Human Rights Watch, 1998).

S

SIERRA LEONE BAR ASSOCIATION (SLBA). (Sierra Leone).
Some African bar associations, including the SLBA, are active in taking up human rights issues. In May 1985, the SLBA called for the establishment of a Human Rights Committee to ensure the protection of human rights and to examine the grounds for executive detention in the country.
Reference: Human Rights Internet, *Human Rights Internet: Reporter* (Boston, MA: Harvard Law School, February 1994).

SOCIETY FOR HUMAN RIGHTS EDUCATION (SAHRE). (Ethiopia).
This is one of the few NGOs in Africa for which education in human rights forms its main strategy. The group began to operate in early 1994, but it could not be effective because of the shortage of funds and bureaucratic caution.
Reference: Claude E. Welch, Jr., *Protecting Human Rights in Africa* (Philadelphia: University of Pennsylvania, 1995).

SOCIETY FOR THE PROTECTION OF HUMAN RIGHTS (SFPHR). (Sierra Leone).
There are constitutional safeguards against arbitrary detention and unjust arrest in Sierra Leone. But in most cases, especially in political and security cases, police and security agencies have additional rights of detention. The government provides legal representation only in cases of capital offenses. Many

indigent detainees do not know their legal rights. The SFPHR provides some legal counsel to indigent detainees.

Reference: US Department of State, *Country Reports on Human Rights Practices for 1993* (Washington, D.C.: Government Printing Office, 1994).

SOMALI WOMEN'S DEMOCRATIC ORGANIZATION (SWDO). (Somalia).

Founded in 1977, this government-supported organization could maneuver strategies under the banner of equality and justice. Ordinary women came to the organization asking its leaders to intervene on their behalf where the court or an employer had proved unfair. One important aim of the SWDO was to fight against genital mutilation, which was still widespread. Currently, the SWDO tries to break the taboos and secrecy surrounding this issue by using education programs on radio and film. Its campaign has been nation-wide. With the blessing of the government, this NGO has proclaimed the goal of eradicating female circumcision by the year 2000.

References: Dahabo Farah Hassan et al., "Somalia: Poetry as Resistance against Colonialism and Patriarchy," in Saskia Wieringa (ed.), *Subversive Women: Historical Experiences of Gender and Resistance* (London: Zed Books,1995); Robin Lloyd, "A Campaign to Stop Female Circumcision," *Toward Freedom* 38 (1) (March-April 1989).

SOMALI WOMEN'S MOVEMENT (SWM). (Somalia).

Established in 1967 by educated middle-class women, the SWM's aim is to fight for social and economic rights. Led by wives of leaders of political parties, it voices women's rights. Most of its activities have been in the area of social welfare. One of the expressed grievances was once composed in a for educated readers. It said: "Even the lowest positions were not offered and our degrees were cast aside as dirt." The movement works for women's empowerment.

Reference: US Department of State, *Country Reports on Human Rights Practices for 1993* (Washington, D.C.: Government Printing Office, 1994).

S.O.S.-ESCLAVES. (Mauritania).

Slavery in several forms still exists in the 1990s in Mauritania among the Afro-Mauritanian communities. The S.O.S.-Esclaves was particularly active in drawing public attention to the issue and as such issued a report in 1996 detailing its activities. It did several things. First, it sent requests to international bodies and national governments in the continent to support measures to eradicate slavery. Second, it intervened effectively with the Mauritanian authorities to push resolution of some cases, in particular child custody cases that were brought to the organization by former slaves. Third, partly at its request, various international bodies, such as the Pan-African Gerdes-Africa or International Study and Research Group on Democracy and Economic and Social Development in Africa, established a branch in Mauritania to address human rights issues concerning slavery in Mauritania.

Reference: US Department of State, *Country Reports on Human Rights Practices for 1993* (Washington, D.C.: Government Printing Office, 1994).

S.O.S. WOMEN. (Mauritius).

Women do not get equal treatment in Mauritius, and in fact there is no specific body of law mandating equal treatment of women in work places. Nor are there any laws relating to sexual harassment of women. Moreover, women cannot transmit citizenship to their foreign born children. Spousal abuses go mostly unnoticed. The S.O.S. Women, an NGO, provides assistance to abused women and sensitizes the Mauritian population to women's rights. In 1993, the group claimed that it had contacted about 150 abused women each month.

Reference: US Department of State, *Country Reports on Human Rights Practices for 1993* (Washington, D.C.: Government Printing Office, 1994).

SOUTH AFRICAN CAMPAIGN TO BAN LANDMINES. (South Africa).

In the early 1990s, NGOs brought the landmines crisis to the attention of the public. In southern Africa, various coalitions of NGOs have formed national campaigns to ban landmines as part of the International Campaign to Ban Landmines. The oldest campaign is the South African Campaign to Ban Landmines, which began operation in July 1995.

Reference: Human Rights Watch, *Still Killing: Landmines in Southern Africa* (New York: Human Rights Watch, 1997).

SOUTH AFRICAN PRISONERS ORGANIZATION FOR HUMAN RIGHTS (SAPOHR). (South Africa).

This pressure group was organized by ex-prisoners. It embarked on strikes in support of the prisoners' claim to political status. In 1993, it organized widespread strikes in prisons for prison reforms.

Reference: Africa Watch, *Prison Conditions in South Africa* (New York: Human Rights Watch, 1994).

STUDY AND RESEARCH GROUP ON DEMOCRACY (SRGD). (Benin).

This NGO monitors human rights abuses in Benin. It has asked President Soglo to install the Constitutional Court early to deal with cases of civil rights violations. The government has welcomed the groups' scrutiny of human rights.

Reference: US Department of State, *Country Reports on Human Rights Practices for 1993* (Washington, D.C.: Government Printing Office, 1994).

SUDAN CATHOLIC BISHOPS CONFERENCE (SCBC). (Sudan).

Since the 1989 coup, the Sudanese government stamped out any domestic criticism of human rights issues. Almost all of the relatively few local independent human rights monitors have been arrested. The SCBC continued to seek to monitor and publicize human rights abuses, especially those involving religious discrimination.

Reference: US Department of State, *Country Reports of Human Rights Practices for 1993* (Washington, D.C.: Government Printing Office, 1994).

SUDAN COUNCIL OF CHURCHES (SCC). (Sudan).

Since the military coup of 1989, the central government in Sudan discriminated against people on the basis of religion. Christians were mistreated. The SCC monitors these abuses and publicizes cases of discrimination.

Reference: US Department of State, *Country Reports of Human Rights Practices for 1993* (Washington, D.C.: Government Printing Office, 1994).

SUDAN HUMAN RIGHTS ORGANIZATION (SHRO). (Sudan).

First founded in 1984, the SHRO was among several civic groups that were banned following the June 1989 military coup in Sudan. It began its work in December 1991 from London. It participated in the first General Assembly of the **Arab Organization for Human Rights** held in Khartoum in January 1987. Basically, the SHRO argues that the national question can be dealt with properly only when the rights of indigenous and former colonial peoples are treated on their own merits rather than as part of an external power's interest in the region. The human rights dimension of this external problem grew enormously, with millions of refugees fleeing state-sponsored violations of basic rights. In January 1992, the SHRO launched a monthly magazine called *Sudan Human Rights Voice*. This NGO should not be confused with the governmental organization of the same name. Currently, the SHRO campaigns against rights violations through media and conferences, and it offers some human rights training. In 1991, the Sudanese government created another SHRO to defend its human rights record. This government-sponsored organization has yet to criticize the government.

References: Human Rights Internet, *Human Rights Internet: Reporter* (Boston, MA: Harvard Law School, February 1994); George W. Shepherd, Jr., and Mark O. C. Anikpo (eds.), *Emerging Human Rights* (Westport, CT: Greenwood Press, 1990); Human Rights Internet, *Sudan: Chronology of Events, 1993-1995* (Ottawa, Canada: Human Rights Internet, August 1995).

SUDANESE BAR ASSOCIATION (SBA). (Sudan).

Throughout the Nimeiri government, the SBA protested against numerous violations of human rights. Several members of the association were arrested for their protests. Following the change in government, the SBA and the Faculty of the Khartoum University jointly formed a committee to review Sudanese legislation and to ensure compliance with international human rights conditions. In 1989, the bar association signed a memorandum protesting the suppression of trade unions because it considered some trade union activities as human rights activities.

References: Human Rights Internet, *Human Rights Internet: Reporter* (Boston, MA: Harvard Law School, February 1994); Human Rights

Watch, *The Persecution of Human Rights Monitors* (New York: Africa Watch, 1990).

SUPPORT COMMITTEE. (Mauritania).
>The Support Committee asked for assistance for the wives and orphans of victims of the 1990-91 military purge. Extrajudicial killings, primarily of African-Mauritanians, from past years remained uninvestigated and unresolved. While in military custody in 1990-91, many Halpulaar and Soninke military and civilian personnel, approximately 500, died. Many of them were summarily executed by the military government. The parliament gave general amnesty to many, including numerous military officers who were alleged to have been involved in the killings. The Support Committee asked for accountability.

Reference: US Department of State, *Country Reports on Human Rights Practices for 1993* (Washington, D.C.: Government Printing Office, 1994).

SUPPORT COMMITTEE FOR THE RELEASE OF POLITICAL DETAINEES IN DJIBOUTI. (Djibouti).
>In 1992, this committee's president was Hassan Ali Mohammad, who was arrested for criticizing the government for human rights violations. This group worked for the release of prisoners of conscience and argued against torture of detainees. It noted that the special court was not good for a free trial.

Reference: Amnesty International, *The 1993 Report on the Human Rights Around the World* (New York: Hunter House, 1993).

SWAZILAND ACTION GROUP AGAINST ABUSE (SAGAA). (Swaziland).
>Physical abuse of women, particularly wife beating, is common. Women have the right to complain, but the traditional courts are unsympathetic to "unruly" and "disobedient" women. Modern courts are unlikely to punish any husband for wife beating. The SAGAA has established relations with other civic organizations, as well the government, to provide forums to discuss spousal and child abuse, and to educate the people and public on the rights of victims.

Reference: US Department of State, *Country Reports on Human Rights Practices for 1993* (Washington, D.C.: Government Printing Office, 1994).

T

TANZANIA HUMAN RIGHTS EDUCATION SOCIETY.
(Tanzania).

The international NGOs are welcome, but the government refuses to register the Education Society's application for registration because of the suspicion that it has worked to monitor abuses.

Reference: US Department of State, *Country Reports on Human Rights Practices for 1996* (Washington, D.C.: Government Printing Office, 1997).

TOGOLESE LEAGUE OF HUMAN RIGHTS (TLHR). (Togo).

The general public and students suffered gross discriminations under the regime of President General Gnassingbe Eyadema. During 1990, there had been increasing demands for greater respect for human rights and freedom of expression and association. The TLHR reported in November 1990 that five of the political detainees had been tortured by the state police. This report was published in the country's first independent newspaper, *Forum Hebdo*. This compelled the governmental Human Rights Commission to take some action. After the Commission's report, the country's police chief was dismissed. Shortage of qualified judges created a backlog of prisoners who had been held for long periods, at times up to 2 years in detention before being brought to trial. At times, political prisoners were tortured in detention. Alessi Wilson, the treasurer of the TLHR, was held by the security police for more than 48 hours in 1993 because of his investigation of the killings of political prisoners. The TLHR prepared a report in 1993 on the Togolese human rights situation. However, President G. Eyadema-controlled security forces subjected human rights groups to threats and harassment. Many members of the TLHR left Togo. The chief argument of the society was that most prisoners were mere prisoners of conscience.

Reference: Human Rights Watch / Africa Watch, *Academic Freedom and Human Rights Abuses in Africa* (New York: Human Rights Watch, April 1991).

TUNISIAN ASSOCIATION OF DEMOCRATIC WOMEN. (Tunisia).

This independent group issues reports on Tunisia's bad human rights record. It asks for release of prisoners of conscience. When the group wanted to send representatives to a human rights conference in Strasbourg in June 1997, the government pressured the association not to send any one.

Reference: Human Rights Watch, *World Report 1998* (New York: Human Rights Watch, 1998).

TUNISIAN HUMAN RIGHTS LEAGUE. (Tunisia).

Hundreds of prisoners of conscience were arrested during 1995 on suspicion of supporting unauthorized political opposition parties. This NGO monitors prisoners of conscience and reports on torture and ill-treatment of arrested persons. Khemais Ksila, a vice president of the Tunisian Human Rights League, was arrested in September 1997, the day he launched a well-publicized hunger strike to dramatize the price he himself had paid for his human rights work — dismissal from his public-sector job, ban on his travel abroad, and police surveillance. The League continues to speak out against human rights violations through communiqués.

References: Amnesty International, *The 1996 Report of Human Rights Around the World* (New York: Hunter House Publishers, 1996); Human Rights Watch, *World Report 1998* (New York: Human Rights Watch, 1998).

U

UGANDA ASSOCIATION OF WOMEN LAWYERS (FIDA).
(Uganda).

This association of educated women practicing public-interest law, works from its offices in Kampala. This group had already done several positive things to enhance women's and children's rights. First, it advocated for women's training, basing its calculation on the assumption that if women knew the law, they would use it to affect change in their daily life, confronting oppressive state laws and traditional customs that had so far resulted in women's subordinate status in society. To enhance women's rights, the FIDA targeted areas such as marriage, divorce, child custody, property rights during marriage, and inheritance. It sought to increase child-support payments in cases of separation. More significantly, it called for common criminal codes for men and women in Uganda. In March 1988, the association opened a legal clinic to help individual Ugandans, especially women and children. Second, it emphasized economic development as a means of women's equal rights. It focused on legal literacy training for village women. The FIDA carried a project in writing wills to strengthen women's inheritance rights for economic empowerment. In 1988 its legal-aid clinic defended women who faced the loss of property or children because of widowhood or divorce. All these were targeted because the association wished to empower women. By August 1990, the

women's clinic, organized by the group, handled about 1,000 cases dealing with property rights, inheritance, and business concerns. During 1992-95, it undertook a three-year research and law reform program focusing on women.
Reference: Rita M. Byrnes (ed.), *Uganda: A Country Study* (Washington, D.C.: Government Printing Office, 1992).

UGANDA COUNCIL OF WOMEN (UCW). (Uganda).
Before independence, this council of women in Uganda asked for social and legal reforms to improve women's status. In 1960, it passed resolutions to codify customary laws regarding marriage, divorce, and inheritance. In the 1970s, the council pressed for legal reforms that would grant all women the right to own property and retain custody of children after divorce. Influenced by the council, the Museveni government pledged in the late 1980s to eliminate legal discrimination against women.
Reference: Rita M. Byrnes (ed.), *Uganda: A Country Study* (Washington, D.C.: Government Printing Office, 1992).

UGANDA HUMAN RIGHTS ACTIVISTS (UHRA). (Uganda).
Since the early 1980s, the UHRA has monitored political abuses in Uganda through its quarterly publication, *The Activists*. Initially, the UHRA's relations with the Kampala government were tense after the arrest of the UHRA Secretary General Paulo Muwanga, who compared the government's human record to that of the repressive Idi Amin regime. Muwanga was subsequently released, and a UHRA report in 1990 generally approved of President Museveni's human rights record. This organization should not be confused with "Uganda Human Rights Committee," which was set up by President Idi Amin in 1978. Gradually, the UHRA began to concentrate on prison conditions. In late 1986, the group charged that the authorities had imprisoned 10,000 people at the Murchison Bay prison in western Uganda. The group, along with Amnesty International, claimed that prisoners lived in abominable conditions. Currently, the UHRA is moving toward an educational role in sponsoring seminars on human rights and defending the independence of the judiciary.
Reference: Rita M. Byrnes (ed.), *Uganda: A Country Study* (Washington, D.C.: Government Printing Office, 1992).

UGANDA LAW SOCIETY (ULS). (Uganda).

This association of lawyers is one of the most active rights organizations in Uganda. In 1990, about 200 legal practitioners belonged to the ULS. It asked for an independent judiciary and an end to illegal arrests and detention. The ULS defended political figures indicted by the government for political beliefs. It declared that it had no faith in President Museveni's creation, the "Ugandan Human Rights Commission". With its limited funds for operations, it remained passive at times. However, it was active in northern and eastern Uganda, and frequently spoke against human rights violations. Lack of funds and resources hampered the ULS's activities. It now operates legal aid clinics in four regional offices. The ULS assists both military and civil defendants.

Reference: Rita M. Byrnes (ed.), *Uganda: A Country Study* (Washington, D.C.: Government Printing Office, 1992).

UGANDA PEOPLE'S DEMOCRATIC MOVEMENT (UPMD). (Uganda).

This opposition political movement in Uganda corroborated evidence of atrocities and abuses acquired by Amnesty International. Its secretary general, Dr. H. Benjamin Obonyo, charged that the government burned or buried civilians alive to crush political dissents. The movement has been active in northern and eastern Uganda.

Reference: Rita M. Byrnes (ed.), *Uganda: A Country Study* (Washington, D.C.: Government Printing Office, 1992).

UGANDA PRISONERS' AID FOUNDATION (UPAF). (Uganda).

Media access to prisons remained limited in Uganda. This foundation monitors prison conditions, but because the prison visits required prior permission from Ugandan authorities, the foundation could do little to inspect the prisons.

Reference: US Department of State, *Country Reports on Human Rights Practices for 1994* (Washington, D.C.: Government Printing Office, 1995).

UNDUGU SOCIETY OF KENYA (USK). (Kenya).

This NGO speaks against violence committed against street kids all over Kenya. Violence, committed by police against young boys and girls, increased in the 1990s. This private organization argued that there should be strict accountability of law enforcement personnel. Often, police used lethal force because they viewed street children as hardened criminals and as such treated them with severity. Police also abused and exploited children for their own personal gain. Girls in Nairobi were reported to have been sexually propositioned or coerced into having sex with police. The USK complained against these abuses.

Reference: Human Rights Watch, *Juvenile Injustice: Police Abuse and Detention of Street Children in Kenya* (New York: Human Rights Watch, 1997).

UNION FOR DEMOCRACY AND SOCIAL PROGRESS (UDPS).
(Democratic Republic of Congo, formerly Zaire).

This private group reports on inhuman treatment and torture of political dissidents. In 1996, it reported that two of its members were tortured by the government Civil Guard because of different political beliefs.

Reference: US Department of State, *Country Reports on Human Rights Practices for 1996* (Washington, D.C.: Government Printing Office, 1997).

UNIVERSAL DEFENDERS OF DEMOCRACY. (Nigeria).

This prodemocracy organization monitors human rights violations in Nigeria. In 1993, its president, Chief Mike Ozehkhome, a lawyer, was detained because he asked for free and fair elections. This NGO works in cooperation with the Committee for the Defense of Human Rights and the Campaign for Democracy.

Reference: Lawyers Committee for Human Rights, *In Defense of Rights: Attacks on Lawyers and Judges in 1993* (New York: Lawyers Committee for Human Rights, 1993).

UNIVERSITY OF BOTSWANA LEGAL ASSISTANCE CENTER.
(Botswana).

Poor police training and poor communications in rural areas made it difficult for detainees to obtain legal assistance. The government did not provide any legal assistance to the poor, except in capital punishment cases. This group provided legal assistance to the indigent.

Reference: US Department of State, *Country Reports on Human Rights Practices for 1996* (Washington, D.C.: Government Printing Office, 1997).

V

VOICE OF THE VOICELESS FOR HUMAN RIGHTS.
(Democratic Republic of Congo, formerly Zaire).

This is an active Zairian league for human rights. It operated relatively freely in the past and was not harassed by the government, although the group occasionally criticized the government's human rights record. President Mobutu, however, refused to give any official permission to investigate human rights abuses. When President Kabila took over the presidency, the Voice of the Voiceless became a target of governmental attack. This NGO claims that in March 1998, government soldiers attacked Floribert Chebeya, president of the group. It argues that the recent campaign of hatred by the government media has created tension between this group and the authorities. It has called for an urgent measure to guarantee the Voice of the Voiceless and other organizations the conditions necessary to enable them to carry out their activities for the promotion and defense of human rights and fundamental liberties. Now it reports on the government's repressive policy toward human rights defenders. In 1997, this organization reported that the main culprits for security in all eleven regions were the undisciplined soldiers.

References: Sandra W. Meditz (ed.), *Zaire: A Country Study* (Washington, D.C.: Government Printing Office, 1994); The Human Rights Actions Network, www.derecho.org/human-rights/actions/

W

WOMEN AGAINST WOMEN ABUSE (WAWA). (South Africa).
This contact group provides relief to battered women in South Africa. This nongovernmental body's efforts, although at times hampered by limited resources as well as race, class, and other divisions between women's groups, have resulted in many positive results.
Reference: Human Rights Watch / Africa Watch, *Violence Against Women in South Africa* (New York: Human Rights Watch, 1995).

WOMEN FOR DEVELOPMENT AND ENTERPRISE IN AFRICA. (Senegal).
Women in the countryside do all the farm work, but have only limited opportunities for an education. This new group works for women's economic empowerment.
Reference: US Department of State, *Country Reports on Human Rights for 1993* (Washington, D.C.: Government Printing Office, 1994).

WOMEN IN LAW AND DEVELOPMENT (WILDAF). (USA).
In a few countries in Africa there are private organizations called WILDAF, which focus on legal education, training, and rights awareness at the grassroots level. It also is concerned with violence against women and the trafficking of women. The organization addresses women's issues at both national and regional levels. WILDAF has identified four common legal problem areas for women in Africa: family, property,

employment, and violence. However, the group has not effectively implemented its objectives in Africa. There are problems of inadequate funding as well as deficiency in group dynamics.

Reference: Women in Law and Development Africa, *WILDAF: Origins and Issues* (Washington, D.C.: OEF International, 1990).

WOMEN IN LAW AND DEVELOPMENT (WILDAF). (Zimbabwe). According to this women's organization, domestic violence accounts for more than 60 percent of murder cases in the Harare High Court. The group argues that despite legal prohibitions, women in Zimbabwe are still vulnerable to entrenched customary harmful practices.

Reference: US Department of State, *Country Reports on Human Rights Practices for 1996* (Washington, D.C.: Government Printing Office, 1997).

WOMEN IN LAW AND DEVELOPMENT IN AFRICA (WILDAF). (Senegal).
The 1985, the Nairobi conference on women presented the idea of a women's organization to implement regional strategies that had been adopted at the conference. In 1990, 65 women from 16 countries met in Zimbabwe to start WILDAF, a Pan-African women's rights network. The **FEDDAF**, the Senegalese section of WILDAF, was registered as an NGO in 1992. The WILDAF hoped to reinforce the programs on women's rights at the national and regional levels to defend women's rights through the dissemination of educational materials and information on laws, lobbying, and mobilization of women, and the training of paralegals. The **FEDDAF** provides legal aid and training to women. Earlier it took part in the March 8 International Women's Day Celebrations.

References: Swedish NGO Foundation for Human Rights, *The Status of Human Rights Organizations in Sub-Saharan Africa* (Stockholm: International Human Rights Internship Program Publications, 1994); Brendalyn P. Ambrose, *Democratization and the Protection of Human. Rights in Africa: Problems and Prospects* (Westport, CT: Praeger, 1995).

WOMEN IN NIGERIA (WIN). (Nigeria).
WIN was one of the eight large organizations in Nigeria that

worked for human rights, especially women's rights, during the Babangida administration. Now it works under the umbrella organization, the **Campaign for Democracy**. In asking for the restoration of the popular government instead of military rule, it seeks to restore human rights in Nigeria. Glory Afi-Kilanko, President of WIN, declared that "political poverty" was created by leaders. The association had connections with the Federation of Ogoni Women in Nigeria.

References: Claude E. Welch, Jr., *Protecting Human Rights in Africa: Roles and Strategies of Non-Governmental Organizations* (Philadelphia: University of Pennsylvania Press, 1995); Human Rights Watch, *Nigeria* (New York: Human Rights Watch, 1996).

WOMEN LIVING UNDER MUSLIM LAW. (Algeria).

This NGO examines the actions of social forces that use religious principles as instruments of repression against women in Algeria. The main thrust of the society is to appraise strategies that women under fundamentalism can adopt to combat repressive state and customary laws in Muslim societies.

Reference: Brendalyn P. Ambrose, *Democratization and the Protection of Human Rights in Africa: Problems and Prospects* (Westport, CT: Praeger, 1995).

WOMEN ORGANIZED FOR A MORALLY ENLIGHTENED NATION. (Sierra Leone).

Sierra Leone does not recognize domestic violence against women as a societal problem. Women do not have equal access to education and economic opportunities. At the university level, men predominate. The Women Organized for a Morally Enlightened Nation, a local NGO, seeks to educate women throughout the country on their civic duties as well as human rights.

Reference: US Department of State, *Country Reports on Human Rights Practices for 1996* (Washington, D.C.: Government Printing Office, 1997).

WOMEN, LAW AND DEVELOPMENT ASSOCIATION (MULEIDE). (Mozambique).

With the support of international NGOs and with freedom of association guaranteed by the new Constitution in

Mozambique, this nongovernmental organization has been working for about three years. It is concerned with not only with "empowering women" in economic fields, but also with placing emphasis on constitutionality and law. The MULEIDE conducts public education campaigns and provides legal assistance in cases of divorce and separation. It has played a significant role in campaigning for the National Assembly of the Republic to ratify the Convention on the Elimination of all Forms of Discrimination Against Women.

Reference: University of Minnesota Human Rights Library, "Human Rights," http://www.umn.edu/humanrts/africa/mozambique.htm

WOMEN, RIGHTS, AND DEVELOPMENT. (Senegal).

The government of Senegal has modified family matters, and new laws have been adopted by the National Assembly in 1988. These laws reinforced women's rights to divorce, alimony, child support, and employment, but such laws were not effectively enforced, especially in rural areas. This group asked for equal treatment of women.

Reference: US Department of State, *Country Reports on Human Rights for 1993* (Washington, D.C.: Government Printing Office, 1994).

WOMEN'S ACTION GROUP (WAG). (South Africa).

Founded in 1984, this group had been concerned with health, religion, welfare, and community organization. Now it meets regularly to educate women about battering and to share information about women's role in prevention of abuses. It has a counseling service.

Reference: Janice Wood Wetzel, *The World of Women: In Pursuit of Human Rights* (New York: New York University Press, 1993).

WOMEN'S DEFENCE OF THE CONSTITUTIONAL LEAGUE. (South Africa).

In the 1950s apartheid imposed new restrictions on African women. They had to work in towns but faced pass laws, which required them to carry passes to be in white-occupied areas. The Women's Defence of the Constitutional League was founded in 1954, first to demonstrate against pass laws and later to assist pass-law violators. Later, this group was renamed **Black Sash**, which set up **Advice Offices** to help the victims of pass-laws in South Africa.

Reference: Rita M. Byrnes (ed.), *South Africa: A Country Study* (Washington, D.C.: Government Printing Office, 1997).

WOMEN'S DEVELOPMENT ASSOCIATION OF LIBERIA.
(Liberia).

Both the central government and the faction leaders in Liberia's civil war have worked against the restoration of civil society. This society has asked the civil war leaders to disarm and work toward peace. It presumes that continued civil war has contributed to violations of civil rights.

Reference: US Department of State, *Country Reports on Human Rights Practices for 1996* (Washington, D.C.: Government Printing Office, 1997).

WOMEN'S HEALTH RESEARCH NETWORK IN NIGERIA (WHERIN). (Nigeria).

The WHERIN is an empowering society asking for more rights for women. In Nigeria, it runs workshops and seminars to help women with sexual problems, and it advocates on behalf of women. It addresses women's issues both locally and nationally.

Reference: Brendalyn P. Ambrose, *Democratization and the Protection of Human Rights in Africa: Problems and Prospects* (Westport, CT: Praeger, 1995).

WOMEN'S UNION (WU). (Sudan).

The WU is essentially an urban and middle class organization devoted to women's special rights. It was most active during the 1960s when women gained their right to vote and the right of equal pay for equal work. In the aftermath of the destruction of military rule, the principal challenge faced by the WU was how to transform itself from an underground secret organization into a public one to monitor rights status. It remained a vanguard for the women's movement, and it hoped to wipe out all the wrongs perpetuated by 16 years of military rule. Some aspects of the ideology adopted by the WU contained ambiguous positions on women's status in society in Sudan.

References: Zeinab Bashir El Bakri, "The Crisis in the Sudanese Women's Movement," in Saskia Wieringa (ed.), *Subversive Women: Historical Experiences of Gender and Resistance* (London: Zed Books,

1995); Dahabo Farah Hassan et al., "Somalia: Poetry as Resistance against Colonialism and Patriarchy," in Sakia Wieringa (ed.), *Subversive Women: Historical Experiences of Gender and Resistance* (London: Zed Books, 1995).

Z

ZAIRIAN ASSOCIATION FOR THE DEFENSE OF HUMAN RIGHTS (AZADHO). (Democratic Republic of Congo, formerly Zaire).

This group has been allowed to operate freely in Zaire, although it has complained against the Mobutu government's political imprisonment and the lack of people's religious freedom. In September 1993, when it published critical and damaging reports on the government's attitude on human rights issues, the Justice Ministry Officials threatened the AZADHO with closure on the grounds that some of its branch offices were not formally registered. For its part, the AZADHO argued that its application for registration had been delayed because of the government's reluctance to cooperate on some human rights issues. In 1995, the AZADHO members in different parts of Zaire were threatened and attacked by both local officials and the military. According to a report by the AZADHO, government soldiers killed hundreds of fleeing civilians in November 1996; Zairian planes bombed civilians in Goma in February 1997.

References: Sandra W. Meditz (ed.), *Zaire: A Country Study* (Washington, D.C.: Government Printing Office, 1994); US Department of State, *Country Reports on Human Rights for 1993* (Washington, D.C.: Government Printing Office, 1994); Human Rights Watch, *Zaire* (New York: Human Rights Watch, 1997).

ZAIRIAN ELECTOR'S LEAGUE. (Democratic Republic of Congo, formerly Zaire).

This monitoring group checks on the conduct and management of general elections. It asks for free elections and general observances of human rights in Zaire.

Reference: US Department of State, *Country Reports on Human Rights for 1993* (Washington, D.C.: Government Printing Office, 1994).

ZAIRIAN LEAGUE OF HUMAN RIGHTS (LIZADHO).
(Democratic Republic of Congo, formerly Zaire).

Since 1990 several NGOs have been active in monitoring human rights issues. During the early 1990s, the LIZADHO investigated rights abuses and issued reports on the government's attitudes regarding its responsibilities to protect these rights and to meet the basic political rights of the population. Representatives of the LIZADHO, deemed politically sensitive, were prevented from leaving Zaire in the first half of 1993. The Mobutu regime never permitted citizens to freely practice civil and political rights. Some 60,000 Zairians sought political asylum in neighboring countries. This group is concerned with these affairs and occasionally publishes reports about abuses of rights.

Reference: US Department of State, *Country Reports on Human Rights for 1993* (Washington, D.C.: Government Printing Office, 1994).

ZAIRIAN PRISON FELLOWSHIP. (Democratic Republic of Congo, formerly Zaire).

Prison conditions under President Mobutu were very bad. This small group reported about these conditions.

Reference: US Department of State, *Country Reports on Human Rights for 1993* (Washington, D.C.: Government Printing Office, 1994).

ZAMBIA CAMPAIGN TO BAN LANDMINES. (Zambia).

The Zambian government has generally been quiet on the landmines issue, saying that it was not a priority. In September 1996, a group of students and staff at Lusaka's University Teaching Hospital launched the Zambia Campaign to Ban Landmines in an effort to lobby the government and raise pubic awareness of Zambia's as well as South Africa's landmine problems. Members of the campaign included the

Zambia Red Cross Society, medical students, and various NGOs.

Reference: Human Rights Watch, *Still Killing: Landmines in Southern Africa* (New York: Human Rights Watch, 1997).

ZAMBIA CIVIC EDUCATION ASSOCIATION (ZCEA). (Zambia).

This Zambian human rights and civic association generally operates without government interference. However, at times the government claims that the private group over-reports police brutalities.

Reference: US Department of State, *Country Reports on Human Rights for 1993* (Washington, D.C.: Government Printing Office, 1994).

ZAMBIA INDEPENDENT MONITORING TEAM (ZIMT). (Zambia).

This private group had been monitoring elections in Zambia and expressed doubts about free and fair elections. The government charged that the group had obtained assistance from outside sources. In November 1997, the government raided the Lusaka office of the group and seized bank accounts and files, which have never been returned. The group continues to operate in favor of free expression of speech and freedom of action.

Reference: Human Rights Watch, *World Report 1998* (New York: Human Rights Watch, 1998).

ZIMBABWE CAMPAIGN TO BAN LANDMINES. (Zimbabwe).

The Zimbabwe National Army maintains a stock of mines, including anti-personnel mines. On October 3, 1996, a group of concerned individuals, private citizens, workers, academics, and journalists formed this NGO to lobby government officials. It did several things to ban mines. First, it held press conferences for greater media attention. Second, it toured the ZDI mines factory in Domboshwa in Zimbabwe. This campaign group insisted that even after production had stopped, stockpiles of mines remained intact. Third, it called for a total ban on production, trade, stockpiling, and use of mines.

Reference: Human Rights Watch, *Still Killings* (New York: Human Rights Watch, 1997).

ZIMBABWE HUMAN RIGHTS ASSOCIATION (ZIMRIGHTS).
(Zimbabwe).

Police brutality remained a problem in Zimbabwe. The ZIMRIGHTS alleged that there were several disappearances in 1990. Rural dwellers reported that government agents told them that they would not be eligible to receive drought relief if they supported the opposition. The ZIMRIGHTS expressed concern over allegations of intimidation by the security forces of an independent candidate in the Matobo by election.

Reference: US Department of State, *Country Reports on Human Rights for 1993* (Washington, D.C.: Government Printing Office, 1994).

ZIMBABWE UNIVERSITY LAW DEPARTMENT (ZULD).
(Zimbabwe).

In 1983, the Law Department organized an international seminar that led to the creation of a Legal Resources Foundation, which provided basic legal materials for the public, and research into particular problems on human rights. In 1984, members of the Law Department brought an important case to the Supreme Court of Zimbabwe on the legal status of women following the introduction of the Legal Age of Majority Act. This had a considerable effect because it clarified the fact that women from the age of 18 had been given a significant improvement in their status by that Act.

Reference: International Commission of Jurists, *Human and Peoples' Rights in Africa and The African Charter* (Geneva, Switzerland: International Commission of Jurists, 1986).

ZONTA CLUB OF ACCRA (ZCA). (Ghana).

This is a private women's group working on the principle of the right to development. This emerging human rights club has adopted a village in Ghana and is in the process of trying to sink a well to provide clean drinking water. It also has built, among others, a multi-purpose center in the village to house classes on prenatal care, postnatal care, childbirth, and literacy.

Reference: George W. Shepherd, Jr., and Mark O. Oc. Anikpo (eds.), *Emerging Human Rights: The African Political Economy Context* (Westport, CT: Greenwood Press, 1990).

APPENDIX I: AFRICAN STATES WITH CONSTITUTIONAL HUMAN RIGHTS PROVISIONS

1. Algeria (The People's Democratic Republic of)
2. Angola (The Republic of)
3. Benin (The People's Republic of)
4. Botswana (The Republic of)
5. Burkina Faso
6. Burundi (The Republic of)
7. Cameroon (The Republic of)
8. Cape Verde (The Republic of)
9. Central African Republic
10. Chad (The Republic of)
11. Comoros (The Islamic Federal Republic of the)
12. Congo (The Republic of the)
13. Democratic Republic of Congo (formerly Zaire)
14. Djibouti (The Republic of)
15. Egypt (The Arab Republic of)
16. Equatorial Guinea (The Republic of)
17. Eritrea
18. Ethiopia (The Federal Democratic Republic of)
19. Gabon (The Gabonese Republic)
20. Gambia (The Republic of the)
21. Ghana (The Republic of Ghana)
22. Guinea (The Republic of)
23. Guinea-Bissau (The Republic of)
24. Ivory Coast (The Republic of)
25. Kenya (The Republic of)
26. Lesotho (The Kingdom of)
27. Liberia (The Republic of)
28. Libya (The Socialist People's Libyan Arab Jamahiriya)
29. Madagascar (The Democratic Republic of)
30. Malawi (The Republic of)
31. Mali (The Republic of)
32. Mauritania (The Islamic Republic of)
33. Mauritius (The Republic of)
34. Morocco (The Kingdom of) and Western Sahara
35. Mozambique (The Republic of)
36. Namibia
37. Niger (The Republic of)
38. Nigeria (The Federal Republic of)
39. Rwanda (The Rwandese Republic)
40. Sao Tome and Principe (The Democratic Republic of)
41. Senegal (The Republic of)
42. Seychelles (The Republic of)
43. Sierra Leone (The Republic of)
44. Somalia (The Somali

Democratic Republic)
45. South Africa (The Republic of)
46. Sudan (The Republic of the)
47. Swaziland (The Kingdom of)
48. Tanzania (The United Republic of)
49. Togo (The Togolese Republic)
50. Tunisia (The Republic of)
51. Uganda (The Republic of)
52. Zambia (The Republic of)
53. Zimbabwe (The Republic of)

Note: Compiled from Edward Lawson, *Encyclopedia of Human Rights.* New York: Taylor and Francis, 1991.

Appendix II: Human Rights Declarations

1215   Magna Carta (England)
1628   Petition of Rights (England)
1689   Bill of Rights (England)
1776   Virginia Declaration of Rights
1776   American Declaration of Independence (USA)
1789   French Declarations of the Rights of Man and of the Citizen
1948   Universal Declaration of Human Rights (Adopted by UN General Assembly)
1948   American Declaration of the Rights and Duties of Man (Adopted by the Conference of American States)
1949   Basic Law of the Federal Republic of Germany
1950   European Convention for the Protection of Human Rights and Freedoms
1950   Convention Relating to the Status of Refugees (Adopted by UN General Assembly)
1952   Convention on the Political Rights of Women (Adopted by General Assembly, December)
1959   Declaration of the Rights of the Child
1959   American Convention for the Protection of Human Rights and Freedoms
1961   European Social Charter (Turin, Italy)
1965   International Convention on the Elimination of All Forms of Racial Discrimination (Adopted by UN General Assembly)
1966   International Covenant on Economic, Social and Cultural Rights (Adopted by UN General Assembly)
1966   International Covenant on Civil and Political Rights (Adopted by UN General Assembly)
1966   Optional Protocol to the International Covenant on Civil and

	Political Rights (Adopted by General Assembly, December)
1967	Declaration on Territorial Asylum (Adopted by UN General Assembly, December)
1968	Proclamation of Teheran (Proclaimed by the International Conference on Human Rights, May)
1969	Declaration on Social Progress and Development (Proclaimed by UN General Assembly, December)
1974	Universal Declaration on the Eradication of Hunger and Malnutrition
1974	Charter of Economic Rights and Duties of States (Adopted by UN General Assembly)
1975	Final Act of the Conference on Security and Cooperation in Europe
1979	Convention of the Elimination of all Forms of Discrimination Against Women (Adopted by UN General Assembly)
1979	Code on Conduct for Law Enforcement Officials (Adopted by UN General Assembly, December)
1981	African Charter of Human and Peoples' Rights (adopted by the OAU Heads of Governments, at Nairobi, June)
1981	Declaration on the Elimination of All Forms of Intolerance and of Discrimination Based on Religion and Belief (Adopted by UN General Assembly in November, 1981)
1984	Convention Against Torture and Other Cruel, Inhuman or Degrading Treatment of Punishment (Adopted by UN General Assembly)
1985	International Conference of Jurists on The Implementation of Human Rights in Africa (Nairobi Declaration, December 2 — 4, Nairobi)
1988	Khartoum Declaration: Towards a Human Focused Approach to Socio-Economic Recovery and Development in Africa (ECAUN)
1989	Convention on the Rights of the Child (Adopted by UN General Assembly)
1991	Cairo Declaration on Human Rights in Islam
1993	Vienna Conference on Human Rights
1994	Beijing Declaration and Platform for Action (Adopted by Fourth UN World Conference on Women)
1997	International Campaign to Ban Landmines Fourth NGO Conference (Maputu, Mozambique)

BIBLIOGRAPHY

African Human Rights Resource Center. Document on File with the Ministry of Gender and Community Development, Kampala, Uganda, 1995. Home page http://www.umn.edu/humanrts/africa/women.htm

Agbese, Pita O. "The State Versus Human Rights Advocates in Africa: The Case of Nigeria," in Eileen McCarthy-Arnolds, ed., *Africa, Human Rights, and the Global System*. Westport, CT: Greenwood Press, 1994: 146-169.

Aidoo, Akwasi. "Africa: Democracy Without Human Rights?" *Human Rights Quarterly* 15 (1993): 703-715.

Ajomo, M.A. and Isabella Okagbue, eds. *Human Rights and the Administration of Criminal Justice in Nigeria*. Lagos, Nigeria: Nigerian Institute of Advanced Studies, 1991.

Ake, Clude. "Rethinking African Democracy," *Journal of Democracy* 2 (1) (Winter 1991): 32-44.

Alston, Philip. "Economic and Social Rights." In Louis Henkin and John Lawrence Hargrove, eds., *Human Rights: An Agenda for the Next Century*. Washington, D.C.: The American Society of International Law, 1994.

_____. "The Committee on Economic, Social and Cultural Rights." In Philip Alston, ed. *The United Nations and Human Rights: A Critical Evaluation*. Oxford: Clarendon Press, 1992: 473-508.

Ambrose, Brendalyn P. *Democratization and the Promotion of Human Rights in Africa: Problems and Prospects*. Westport, CT: Praeger, 1995.

Amnesty International USA. *The 1993 Report on the Human Rights Around the World*. New York: Amnesty International Publications, 1993.

_____. *Amnesty International: The 1993 Report*. New York: Amnesty International Publications, 1993.

_____. *Amnesty International: The 1994 Report*. New York: Amnesty

African Charter on Human and Peoples' Rights. Document IOR 63/03/93. London: Amnesty International, June 1993.

_____. *Human Rights Violations in Ethiopia.* London: Amnesty International Publications, 1978.

_____. *Torture in the Eighties.* London: Amnesty International, 1984.

Anim, Etim. "Confronting Decree 2," *Newswatch* 13 (August 21, 1989): 3-5.

Ankumah, Evelyn A. *The African Commission on Human and Peoples' Rights: Practices and Procedures.* The Hague: Human Rights Commission, 1996.

An-Na'im, Abdullahi A. ed. *Human Rights in Cross-Cultural Perspectives: A Quest for Consensus.* Philadelphia: University of Pennsylvania Press, 1992.

Arab Organization for Human Rights. "Call for Respect of Human Rights." Giza, Egypt: AOHR, 1995. Home page http://192.203.180.62/mlas/aohr.htm

Bassiouni, M. Cheri, and Ziyad Motala, eds. *The Protection of Human Rights in African Criminal Proceedings.* London: Martinus Publishers, 1995.

Baxter, Paul. "The Problem of the Oromo," in I.M. Lewis, ed. *Nationalism and Self-Determination in the Horn of Africa.* London: Itaca Press, 1983: 129-49. Originally published as "Ethiopia's Unacknowledged Problem: The Oromo," *African Affairs* (1978): 283-96.

Berry, LaVerle, ed. *Ghana: A Country Study.* Washington, D.C.: Government Printing Office, 1995.

Brender, David L. et al. *Human Rights: Opposing Viewpoints.* San Diego, CA: Greenhaven Press, 1998.

Bunch, Charlotte. "Women's Rights as Human Rights: Toward a Re-Vision of Human Rights," *Human Rights Quarterly* 12 (1990): 486-491.

Butegwa, Florence, "The Challenge of Promoting Women's Rights in African Countries." In Joanna Kerri, ed. *Ours By Rights: Women's Rights As Human Rights.* London: Zed Books, 1993: 40-50.

Byrnes, Rita M., ed. *South Africa: A Country Study.* Washington, D.C.: Government Printing Office, 1997.

_____. *Uganda: A Country Study.* Washington, D.C.: Government Printing Office, 1992.

Carver, Rochard and Paul Hunt. "National Human Rights Institutions in Africa." Banjul: African Center for Democracy and Human Rights Studies, 1991.

Center for Human Rights Legal Aid [CHRLA]. "Human Rights." New York. 1997. Home page http:/www.chrla.org/

Charlton, Sue Ellen M. *Women in Third World Development.* Boulder, CO: Westview Press, 1984.

Civil Liberties Organization. *Ajibola Years.* Lagos, Nigeria: Civil Liberties Organization, 1991.

_____. *Behind the Wall: A Report on Prison Conditions in Nigeria and the Nigerian Prison System.* Lagos, Nigeria: Civil Liberties Organization, 1991.

_____. *A Harvest of Violations: Annual Report on Human Rights in Nigeria, 1991.* Lagos, Nigeria: Civil Liberties Organization, 1992.

_____. *Human Rights in Retreat.* Lagos, Nigeria: Civil Liberties Organization, 1993.

_____. *Prisoners in the Shadows: A Report on Women and Children in Five Nigerian Prisons.* Lagos, Nigeria: Civil Liberties Organization, 1993.

Clapman, Christopher. *Africa and the International System.* Cambridge, UK: Cambridge University Press, 1996.

Coalition Against Slavery in Mauritania and Sudan [CASMAS]. 1998. Home page http://www.cc.columbia.edu/-slc11/

Collelo, Thomas, ed. *Angola: A Country Study.* Washington, D.C.: Government Printing Office, 1991.

Cook, Rebecca J., ed. *Human Rights of Women: National and International Perspectives.* Philadelphia: University of Pennsylvania Press, 1994.

Corville, Cindi. *Africa Today* 1 (1990): 23-25.

Days, Drews S. et al. *Justice Enjoined: The State of the Judiciary in Kenya.* New York: Robert Kennedy Memorial Center for Human Rights, 1992.

Deng, Adama, ed. *Paralegals in Rural Africa.* Geneva: International Commission of Jurists, 1991.

Donnelly, Jack. *International Human Rights.* Boulder, CO.: Westview Press, 1993.

Ebiasah, John K. "Protecting the Political Rights of Political Detainees: The Contradictions and Paradoxes in the African Experience." *Howard Law Journal* 22 (3), 1979: 249-281.

Egyptian Organization for Human Rights. *Lawyers Committee for Human Rights: North Africa.* Giza, Egypt: Egyptian Organization for Human Rights, 1991.

El Bakri, Zeinab Bashir. "The Crisis in the Sudanese Women's Movement." In Saskia Wieringa, ed. *Subversive Women: Historical Experiences of Gender and Resistance.* London: Zed Books, 1995.

Ethiopian Human Rights Council. *Special Report 19.* Cairo, Egypt: Human Rights Council, 1997.

Freeman, Marsha A., and A. S. Fraser. "Women's Human Rights: Making the Theory a Reality." In Louis Henkin and John Lawrence Hargrove, eds. *Human Rights: An Agenda for the Next Century.* Washington, D.C.: The American Society of International Law, 1994.

Gaer, Felice D. "First Fruits: Reporting by States under the African Charter on Human and People's Rights." *Netherlands Quarterly of Human Rights* 10 (1), 1992: 9.

Gahia, Chukwuemeka. *Human Rights in Retreat: A Report on the Human Rights Violations of the Military Regime of General Ibrahim Babangida.* Lagos, Nigeria: Civil Liberties Organization, 1993.

Geisler, Gisela. "Troubled Sisterhood." *African Affairs* 94 (1995): 31-34.

Handloff, Robert E., ed. *Cote d'Ivoire: A Country Study.* Washington, D.C.:

Government Printing Office, 1988.

_____. *Mauritania: A Country Study*. Washington, D.C.: Government Printing Press, 1990.

Hansson, Desiree, and Batie Hofmeyr. *Women's Rights: Towards a Non-Sexist South Africa (7)*. Witwatersrand: Center for Legal Studies, Documentation Center, University of Witwatersrand, South Africa, 1992.

Hassan, Dahabo Farah, et. al. "Somalia: Poetry as Resistance against Colonialism and Patriarchy." In Saskia Wieringa, ed. *Subversive Women: Historical Experiences of Gender and Resistance*. London: Zed Books, 1995.

Haynes, Jeff. "Human Rights and Democracy in Ghana." *African Affairs* 3 (1) (1991): 80-83.

Henkin, Louis, and John Lawrence Hargrove, eds. *Human Rights: An Agenda for the Next Century*. Washington, D.C.: The American Society of International Law, 1994.

Houser, George M. *Africa Today* (1992). Home page http://www.derchos.org/human-rights.afr/kenya-1.html

Human Rights Actions Network. "Armed Attack on President of Human Rights Group." Derechos Human Rights, 1998. Home page http://www.derchos.org/human-rights/actions/sos/congo2.html

Human Rights Information and Documentation (HURIDOCS). *Standard Formats: A Tool for Documenting Human Rights Violations*. Geneva: HURIDOCS, 1993.

_____. *Supporting Documents*. Geneva: HURIDOCS, 1993.

Human Rights Internet. *Algeria: Islamism, the State and Armed Conflict*. Ottawa, Canada: University of Ottawa Press, 1995.

_____. *Ghana: Update on the Fourth Republic*. Ottawa, Canada: University of Ottawa Press, 1994.

_____. *Occasional Papers* (Ghana), 1992.

_____. *Reporter*. Boston: Harvard Law School Human Rights Program, February 1989.

_____. *Sudan: Chronology of Events, 1993-1995*. Ottawa, Canada: Human Rights Internet, August, 1995.

Human Rights Library. University of Minnesota, http://www.umn.edu. humanarts/africa/liberia/htm

Human Rights Watch. *Academic Freedom and Human Rights Abuses in Africa*. New York: Human Rights Watch, 1991.

_____. *A Committee on Human Rights Watch, Kenya*. Washington, D.C.: Human Rights Watch, April 1990.

_____. *Accounting in Namibia: Human Rights and the Transition to Democracy*. New York: Human Rights Watch, 1992.

_____. *Angola*. New York: Human Rights Watch, February 1996.

_____. *Divide and Rule, Kenya*. New York: Human Rights Watch, 1993.

_____. *Global Report on Women's Human Rights*. New York: Human Rights Watch, 1995.

_____. *Human Rights Abuses in Algeria: No One is Spared.* New York: Human Rights Watch, 1997.

_____. *Human Rights in Africa and US Policy.* New York: Human Rights Watch, 1997.

_____. *Juvenile Injustice: Police Abuse and Arbitrary Detention of Street Children in Kenya.* New York: Human Rights Watch, 1997.

_____. *Kenya.* http://www.derechos.org/human-rights/afr/kenya-lhtml

_____. *Landmines in Mozambique.* New York: Human Rights Watch, 1997.

_____. *No Neutral Ground: South Africa's Confrontation with Activist Churches.* New York: Human Rights Watch, August 1989.

_____. *Police Abuse and Detention of Street Children.* New York: Human Rights Watch, 1997.

_____. *Prison Conditions in South Africa: Prison Project.* New York: Human Rights Watch, 1994.

_____. *Revolutionary Injustice: Abuses of the Legal System Under the PNDC Government.* New York: Human Rights Watch, 1992.

_____. *Sexual Violence During the Rwandan Crisis.* New York: Human Rights Watch, 1997.

_____. *Shattered Lives: Rwandan Genocide.* New York: Human Rights Watch, 1996.

_____. *Still Killings: Landmines in Southern Africa.* New York: Human Rights Watch, 1997.

_____. *The Ogoni Crisis.* New York: Human Rights/Africa, July 1995.

_____. *The Persecution of Human Rights Monitors.* New York: Africa Watch, 1990.

_____. *Violence Against Women in South Africa.* New York: Human Rights Watch, 1995.

_____. *World Report 1996.* New York: Human Rights Watch, 1996.

_____. *World Report 1997.* New York: Human Rights Watch, 1997.

_____. *World Report 1998.* New York: Human Rights Watch, 1998.

_____. *Zaire: Forced to Flee: Violence Against the Tutsi in Zaire.* New York: Human Rights Watch, 1997.

_____. *Zaire: Inciting Hatred: Violence Against Kasaiens in Shaba.* New York: Human Rights Watch, 1993.

_____. *Zambia.* New York: Human Rights Watch, July 1997.

Ihonvbere, Julius O. "A Critical Evaluation of the Failed 1990 Coup in Nigeria," *Journal of Modern African Studies* 29 (1991): 601-26.

_____. "Are Things Falling Apart?" *Journal of Modern African Studies* 34 (2), 1996.

International Commission of Jurists. *Human and Peoples' Rights in Africa and the African Charter.* Geneva: Centre for the Independence of Judges and Lawyers of the International Commission of Jurists, 1986.

_____. *A Paralegal Trainer's Manual for Africa.* Geneva, Switzerland: International Commission of Justice, 1994.

_____. *Paralegals in Rural Africa.* Geneva: Center for the Independence of Judges and Lawyers of the International Commission of Jurists, 1991.

Irungu, Gathii. "Twenty Years Caring for Justice." *Haki Mail* 1:1 April 1993: 2-5.

Jacobson, Harold K. *Networks of Independence: International Organization and the Global Political System.* New York: Alfred Knopf, 1984.

Kannyo, Edward. "The Banjul Charter on Human and People's Rights: Genesis and Political Background." In Claude E., and Ronald I. Meltzer, eds., *Human Rights and Development in Africa.* Albany: State University of New York Press, 1984: 128-134.

_____. "The OAU and Human Rights." In Yassin El-Ayouty and I. William Zartman, eds., *The OAU After Twenty Years.* New York: Praeger, 1984: 155-72.

Kardi, John. *The Practice of Female Circumcision in the Upper East Region of Ghana.* Accra, Ghana: Ghanaian Association for Women's Welfare, September 1986.

Kenya Human Rights Commission Prisons Project. *A Death Sentence: Prison Conditions in Kenya.* Nairobi, 1994.

Keri, Joanna, ed. *Ours by Right: Women's Rights as Human Rights.* London: Zed Books, 1993.

Lawson, Edward. *Encyclopedia of Human Rights.* New York: Taylor & Francis, 1991.

Lawyers Committee for Human Rights. *Kenya.* February 1992.

_____. *Malawi: Ignoring Calls for Change.* New York: The Lawyers Committee, 1993.

League of Kenya Women Voters. "Human Rights, Kenya." 1998. Home page http://wwww.derechos.org/human-rights/afr/kenya-l.html

Livezey, Lowel W. *Nongovernmental Organizations and the Ideas of Human Rights.* Princeton, NJ: The Center for International Studies, 1988.

Lloyd, Robin. "A Campaign to Stop Female Circumcision." *Toward Freedom,* 38 (1) 1989: 22-25.

MacGaffey, Janet, ed. *The Real Economy of Zaire: The Contribution of Smuggling and Other Unofficial Activities to National Wealth.* Philadelphia: University of Pennsylvania Press, 1991.

M'Baye, Keba. "Emergence of the 'Right to Development' as a Human Right in the Context of a New International Economic Order." UNESCO Doc. SS-78/CONF. 630/8. July 16, 1979.

McCarthy-Arnolds, Eileen et al. *Africa, Human Rights, and the Global System.* Westport, CT: Greenwood Press, 1994.

McQuoid-Masos, David et al. *Human Rights For All.* Pretoria, South Africa: David Philip Publishers, 1991.

Meditz, Sandra W., ed. *Zaire: A Country Study.* Washington, D.C.: Government Press, 1993.

Metz, Helen C., ed. *Algeria: A Country Study.* Washington, D.C.: Government

Printing Office, 1994.

Mgoqui, Wallace. "The Work of the Legal Resources Center in South Africa in the Area of Human Rights Promotion and Protections." *Journal of African Law* 36 (36) (1992): 1-11.

Middle East Watch. *Human Rights Abuses in Algeria: No One is Spared.* New York: Human Rights Watch, 1994.

Mohanty, Chandra Talpade, et al., eds. *Third World Women and the Politics of Feminism.* Bloomington: Indiana University Press, 1991.

Monique Prindezis, ed. *Schools for Peace.* Geneva, Switzerland: EIP, 1996.

Nelson, Harold D., ed. *Mozambique: A Country Study.* Washington, D.C.: Government Printing Office, 1984.

New Nigerian Youth Movement. *Constitution of Nigerian Youth Movement. Bamako.* May 1998. Home page http://www.uib.no/isf/people/campaign/nnym.htm

Nigerian Federal Ministry of Justice. *Perspectives on Human Rights.* Lagos, Nigeria: Ministry of Justice, 1992.

Nowak, Manfred, and T. Swinhart, ed. *Human Rights in Developing Countries: 1989 Year Book.* Strasbourg, Germany: N.P. Engel Publishers, 1989.

Nzomo, Maria. "The Impact of the Women's Decade on Policies, Programs and Empowerment of Women in Kenya." *Issue* (Summer 1989).

Osaghae, Eghosa A. "The Ogoni Uprising." *African Affairs* 94: 1995.

Parpart, Jane L. "Women and the State in Africa." In Donald Rothchild and Naomi Chazan, eds., *The Precarious Balance: State and Society in Africa.* Boulder, CO: Westview Press, 1988: 208-225.

Raoul Wallenberg Institute. *Human Rights Workshop Namibia.* Lund: The Institute, February 1991.

Rape Crisis. As cited in Desiree Hansson and Batie Hofmeyr. *Women's Rights: Towards a Non-Sexist South Africa*, no. 7, Developing Justice Series. Documentation Center, Center for Legal Studies, University of Witwatersrand, 1992.

Rembe, Nasila Selasini. *Africa and Regional Protection of Human Rights: A Study of the African Charter on Human and Peoples' Rights: Its Effectiveness and Impact on the African States.* Roma, Lesotho: Center for International Juridical Cooperation, 1985.

_____. *The System of Protection of Human Rights Under the African Charter on Human and Peoples' Rights.* Rome: Human Rights Groups, 1991.

Rich, Paul B., ed. *Reaction and Renewal and in South Africa.* New York: St. Martin's Press, 1996.

Richburg, Keith B. *Out of America.* New York: Basic Books, 1997.

Saro-Wiwa, Ken. *Genocide in Nigeria: The Ogoni Tragedy.* London: Saros, 1992.

Schmid, Alex, and Albert J. Jongman, eds. *Monitoring Human Rights Violations.* Leiden: Centre for the Study of Social Conflicts, 1992.

Scoble, Harry M. "Human Rights Non-Governmental Organizations in Black

Africa: Their Problems and Prospects in the Wake of the Banjul Charter."
In Claude E. Welch, Jr. and Ronald I. Meltzer, eds., *Human Rights and
Development in Africa.* Albany: State University of New York Press,
1984: 177-203.

Sen, Gita, and Caren Crown. *Development, Crises, and Alternative Visions.* New
York: Monthly Review Press, 1987.

Shepherd, George W., Jr., and Mark O. Anikpo, eds. *Emerging Human Rights.*
Westport/London: Greenwood Press, 1990.

Shivji, Issa G. *The Concept of Human Rights in Africa.* London: Council for the
Development of Economic and Social Research in Africa [CODESRIA]
Books, 1989.

Sock, Raymond. "The Case for an African Court of Human and Peoples
Rights," *African Topics* March-April, 1994: 3-5.

Staff Reporter, "Voices of Abiya." *West Africa* November 20-28, 1989: 12-13.

Swedish NGO Foundation for Human Rights. *The Status of Human Rights
Organizations in Sub-Saharan Africa.* Stockholm: The International Human Rights Internship Program Publications, 1994.

Umozurike, U. Oji. *The African Charter on Human and Peoples' Rights.* The
Hague/London: 1997.

_____. *Self-Determination in International Law.* Hamden, CT: Archon, 1972.

_____. "The Protection of Human Rights Under the Banjul African Charter
on Human and Peoples' Rights." *African Journal of International Law* 1
(1988): 65-83.

University of Minnesota Human Rights Library. "The Status of Human Rights
Organizations in Sub-Saharan Africa." 1998. Home page http://www.
umn.edu/humanrts/africa/mozambiq.htm.

US Department of State. *Country Reports on Human Rights Practices for 1993.*
Washington, D.C.: Government Printing Office, 1994.

_____. *Country Reports on Human Rights Practices for 1994.* Washington,
D.C: Government Printing Office, 1995.

_____. *Country Reports on Human Rights Practices for 1995.* Washington,
D.C. Government Printing Office, 1996.

_____. *Country Reports on Human Rights Practices for 1996.* Washington,
D.C.: Government Printing Office, 1997.

_____. *Country Reports on Human Rights Practices for 1997.* Washington,
D.C.: Government Printing Office, 1998.

Waltz, Susan. "Making Waves: The Political Impact of Human Rights Groups in
North Africa." *Journal of Modern African Studies* 29, 3 (1991): 481-504.

Welch, Claude E., Jr. "The Ogoni and Self-Determination: Increasing Violence
in Nigeria." *Journal of Modern African Studies* 33 (4) 9 December 1995:
635-650.

_____, ed. *Human Rights in Developing Countries: Problems and Prospects:
Sub-Saharan Africa,* vol. 1. Buffalo: State University of New York Press,
1989.

_____, and R. I. Meltzer, eds. *Human Rights and Development in Africa.* Albany: State University of New York Press, 1984.

Wetzel, Janice Wood. *The World of Women: In Pursuit of Human Rights.* New York: New York University Press, 1993.

Wiseberg, Laurie S. "Human Rights in Africa: Toward a Definition of the Problem of Double Standard." *Issue: A Journal of Africanist Opinion* 6 (4) (1976): 3-13.

Wisemen, John A., ed. *Democracy and Political Change in Sub-Saharan Africa.* London: Routledge, 1995.

Wolde-Mariam, Mesfin. *Suffering Under God's Environment: A Vertical Study of Peasants in North-Central Ethiopia.* Berne, Switzerland: African Mountain Association, Geographica Bernesia, 1991.

Women in Law and Development Africa. *WILDAF: Origins and Issues.* Washington, D.C.: OEF International, 1990.

World Organization Against Torture. "S.O.S.-Torture." Cameroon Actions. 1997. http://www.derechos.org/omct/actions/cmr

SUBJECT INDEX

COUNTRY INDEX

About the Author

SANTOSH SAHA is Assistant Professor of History at Mount Union College in Alliance, Ohio.

ISBN 0-313-30945-0

EAN

9 780313 309458

90000>

HARDCOVER BAR CODE